Ninth Edition W9-BXF-336

SPEAKING WITH A PURPOSE

Arthur Koch
Emeritus, Milwaukee Area Technical College

Jason Schmitt
Green Mountain College

Boston Columbus Indianapolis New York San Francisco Upper Saddle River
Amsterdam Cape Town Dubai London Madrid Milan Munich Paris Montréal Toronto
Delhi Mexico City São Paulo Sydney Hong Kong Seoul Singapore Taipei Tokyo

Editor-in-Chief, Communication: Karon Bowers
Editorial Project Manager: Stephanie Chaisson
Project Manager: Pat Brown
Senior Marketing Manager: Blair Zoe Tuckman
Digital Editor: Lisa Dotson
Art Director, Cover: Jayne Conte
Cover Designer: Karen Salzbach
Cover Photo: Gold Sunrise/Alamy Images
Editorial Production and Composition Service: Sudha Balasundaram/
    S4Carlisle Publishing Services

Library of Congress Cataloging-in-Publication Data

Koch, Arthur, 1931-
    Speaking with a purpose/Arthur Koch; Jason Schmitt.—9th ed.
        p. cm.
    Includes index.
    ISBN-13: 978-0-205-22040-3
    ISBN-10: 0-205-22040-1
    1. Public speaking. I. Schmitt, Jason. II. Title.
    PN4129.15.K62 2013
    808.5'1—dc23
                                        2012026695

1 2 3 4 5 6 7 8 9 10

 www.pearsonhighered.com

ISBN-10:   0-205-22040-1
ISBN-13: 978-0-205-22040-3

*Dedicated to those who work to
improve our environment*

CONTENTS

PREFACE

Numerous rewards await the person who can communicate successfully through speech. Improved self-concept, increased confidence, greater employability, and the ability to get along better with others are just a few of these benefits.

Speaking with a Purpose is designed to help speakers develop the skills they need to prepare and deliver effective speeches. It is geared toward the student who wants practical advice and hands-on experience in speaking. This new edition continues to offer the concise, practical, step-by-step approach to the speechmaking process that has made the book successful through numerous editions.

Speaking with a Purpose is based primarily on a traditional public speaking approach combined with up-to-date communication theory. It is intentionally brief in order to give the reader more time to prepare, practice, and present speeches. The step-by-step approach of the book allows students to concentrate on the speechmaking process.

NEW TO THIS EDITION

Numerous changes have been made to this new edition of *Speaking with a Purpose* to ensure its currency and relevancy to students in today's academic environment. In addition to countless edits, updated examples, and the addition of more current research, the following changes have been made:

- New discussion questions allow students to apply what they learn in the class to situations they experience in daily life.
- Refined, easy to understand language and modern examples make relating to the text easy for a wide variety of students.
- Updated strategies for including new media in speech presentations, such as YouTube videos, help make the skills students learn in this text relevant and applicable to everyday life.
- Chapter 5 provides an updated focus on how to use modern search engines like Google to effectively find pertinent research for presentations.
- Chapter 2 provides a new detailed examination of Maslow's Hierarchy of Needs and its relation to the audience.
- The importance of listening from both an audience and individual standpoint is highlighted, emphasizing the significance of strong listening skills for all aspects of daily life.
- Modernized persuasive speech fundamentals help to place persuasion in a modern scope.
- A focus on food and food allergies and their influence on speech apprehension creates a unique component to this text.
- A new focus on visualization case studies will engage the reader.

Speaking with a Purpose is written in a reader-friendly style. Most reviewers who critiqued the book labeled the readability, writing style, level, and pace of the book as "excellent."

The text contains numerous up-to-date examples that relate to what's going on in the world today. From focusing on better refining Google searches to how to effectively use YouTube in a presentation setting, this text is situated in the current technological landscape. Pictures and graphs have been used sparingly and other visual aids have been kept to a minimum in order to keep the book inexpensive. The arrangement of the book is logical. Chapter 1 discusses the importance of speech, guidelines to successful speechmaking, listening, note taking, projecting confidence, the speech-communication process, and ethics in communication. Chapters 2 through 8 follow a seven-step approach on how to prepare and deliver a successful speech, highlighting the importance of combining personal knowledge and experience with modern technology. Chapter 9 covers speaking to inform and Chapter 10 involves an in-depth study of persuasion and persuasive speaking. Finally, Chapter 11—the group communication chapter—provides the inclusion of such important concepts as group synergy and the various discussion formats students are sure to engage in their professional careers.

We continue to provide an Instructor's Manual to adopters of the text to assist with preparation for the classroom. To download the Instructor's Manual and learn about other supplementary materials, please visit Pearson's Instructor Resource Center at www.pearsonhighered.com/irc (access code required).

We want to thank Teresa Plummer, Marion Technical College, Barbara Rodriguez, Florida National University, Dennis Walker, Northwest Nazarene University, Joe Zubrick, University of Maine—Fort Kent for their valuable suggestions in reviewing this book. Art would like to give a special thanks to Marion Tyndale Carter, Crafton Hills College, California, for her section on controlling nervousness in Chapter 1, and to his ex-wife, Marion, and sons, Carl, Kai, and Christian, for their contributions to this edition. Jason would like to thank his wife Kristen and daughter Bennett for being his unconditional sounding board as well as Joey Reyes for his expertise and help in graphic design. It is also important to thank Sudha Balasundaram, Stephanie Chaisson, and Megan Sweeney for directing and keeping an eye on this text in its many various stages and forms as well as Karon Bowers our editor and the many other people at Pearson who have made this new edition possible.

1 Speech Communication

S peech communication involves the ability to understand and be understood. One of life's most important functions is the ability to communicate effectively with others. Communication gets you hired, makes your ideas more powerful, and allows you to change this world for the better. Becoming a better speaker involves learning to get your ideas across to others in an easy-to-understand, interesting way. *Speaking with a Purpose* is designed to assist you in learning to prepare, organize, and deliver well-received speeches and presentations. Good speakers are not born with the ability to speak effectively; they develop the ability to speak well as the result of commitment and hard work. The key to success in speaking is practice. The more speeches that you prepare and present successfully, the more proficient, relaxed, and confident you will become.

THE COMMUNICATIVE ACT

Communication, at its core, is an amazing process. In a current view, communication is similar to Bluetooth wireless technology between the speaker and the receiver of a message. The speaker can see a beautiful red leather chair, and through descriptive words (which almost act like computer binary), the image of the chair can be passed to the receiver—transferred through words, words that we don't often realize we are deciphering. If the message is passed without any interference, the receiver can now imagine a fairly similar red leather chair to the one that was described.

Becoming a more competent communicator will increase our ability to create more vivid images in the minds of our audiences, coworkers, or bosses. This skill has the opportunity to gives us more clout, a stronger leadership ability, and invariably more power in life.

The study of communication and our speaking ability is not a new phenomenon. Early Greek and Roman empires, at the dawn of time, knew the important components of leadership. These societies taught the up-and-coming leaders math, science, and rhetoric (speech communication). The early foundations of society knew that it wasn't enough just to "know" the information. How we deliver the information is just as pivotal. In a global world coupled with a competitive job climate, our ability to communicate effectively is paramount.

Five elements are involved in the speech communication process: a speaker, a message, a channel (through which the message is sent), an audience, and a response. Each time a speaker communicates a message to others, these elements are present. In speaking situations, these elements interact with each other. A simple speech situation can be summarized as follows:

1. A speaker wishes to communicate an idea. (*I want to sell you a Slap Chop food chopper.*)
2. The speaker encodes the idea in a message. (*I organize my thoughts on its attributes.*)
3. The message is sent through a channel to an audience. (*I present to you how great this item is.*)
4. The audience receives and decodes the message. (*You watch my demonstration and think it looks great.*)
5. The audience responds to the message. (*You go out and buy your very own Slap Chop food chopper.*)

As you can see, the communication process is complex. In order to understand it better, it might be helpful to consider each of the five elements in the process separately.

Speaker

In the previous model, the process of communication begins with a speaker who wishes to communicate an idea or some ideas. The image that the audience has of the speaker affects the message. Those in the audience who perceive a speaker as being competent or full of integrity will be more likely to believe what the speaker says.

Message

The second element in the communication process is the message. In order to ensure that the listener attends to the message and understands it, the speaker must encode it in a language that is both interesting and clear. Emphasis, variety, and descriptive language help make material interesting. Words that are specific and familiar help to make a message clear.

Channel

The channel is the means through which a message is transmitted. In a modern view, the channels for messages to travel through are vast and continuously growing. Facebook, Skype, Twitter, and Reddit all allow messages to be passed from one individual to another as do sign language and ancient smoke signals. In the speaking situation, multiple channels can be involved. Messages can be transmitted through hearing, seeing, smelling, tasting, and touching channels. If you are talking about coffee beans and the smell of the Columbian beans fills the room, it isn't just the verbal message that is conveying the information.

Audience

Without an audience, communication does not take place. A person stranded on an island can put a note in a bottle or stand on the shore screaming for help. However, unless someone reads the note or hears the screams, nothing will have been accomplished. This emphasizes the fact that all communication by a speaker must be directed to an audience.

Response

The success or failure of a communication is determined by audience response. The title of this book, *Speaking with a Purpose*, underlines the fact that in order to be successful when communicating, the speaker's purpose—to inform, to persuade, or to entertain—must be achieved. Therefore, the success or failure of a communication is measured by whether or not those in the audience responded in some way to the message.

COMMUNICATION MODELS

The prior speech communication components are derived from the original study of communication conducted in the 1940s by Claude Shannon who worked at Bell Telephone Company, and Warren Weaver, a mathematician. Together Shannon and Weaver expressed the communication relationship through the following linear model (Figure 1.1).

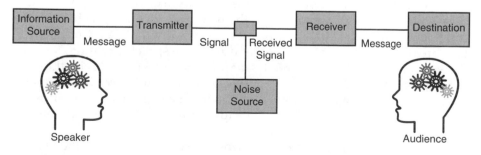

FIGURE 1.1 Communication Model (Linear)

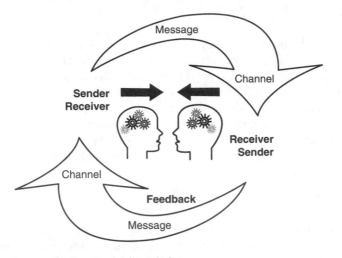

FIGURE 1.2   Communication Model (Circular)

Although Shannon and Weaver received praise for their theory, which seemed to represent how people talk over a telephone, it didn't fit the complexities associated with people as they speak in person. Eventually in the 1960s, the earlier linear model was changed to a cyclical process. By adding the concept of feedback, this new theory took into account that even when you are speaking, your audience is giving messages right back to you (Figure 1.2). The messages that you receive back from your audience (feedback) allow you to adapt to better fit the current environment. The old adage "You cannot not communicate" seems to reference the addition of the feedback loop to the following modern communication model.

COMMUNICATION BREAKDOWNS

Communication breakdowns occur because of some failure in the communication process. If you invite a friend to your house for a Friday night dinner and they come Thursday night, the message you gave them was either inaccurate or misunderstood. If because you were daydreaming you fail to hear your instructor announce that the next class meeting has been called off, you might be the only class member present on that day. Communication breakdowns occur at some point during the speech situation. Perhaps the speaker has failed to correctly analyze the audience. Maybe the message has been encoded in technical terms that the audience cannot understand. Or it might be that the microphone the speaker is using significantly distorts the message. Any of these factors could result in a breakdown of communication.

Usually communication breakdowns can be traced to one of the five elements in the speech communication process: the speaker, message, channel, audience, or response. Consider the following situations and determine where the breakdowns in communication occurred:

1. Some of the members of your audience fail to understand parts of your speech on the addictive nature of the computer game The Sims because of the terminology you use. (Remember, you are most likely to talk to a general audience. What is clear to avid fans of the game might seem like gibberish to those who are not.)
2. What you are wearing draws attention to itself, interfering with your message. (The clothes you wear should not distract or detract from what you are saying. Dressing too flamboyantly or too casually can conflict with what you are saying.)
3. The computer is not recognizing your USB drive. (A good rule when planning to use visual aids in a speech is "be prepared to do without them if need be." An audience will admire the speaker who is able to do this.)
4. The room you are speaking in is large and it is difficult for those in the back to hear you. (If you haven't checked this out beforehand, you can only ask those in the back to move forward or increase your volume.)
5. Some type of external noise interferes with your audience's ability to hear you. (Remain silent until the noise stops. Unless your audience can hear you, communication is not taking place.)

LISTENING

Listening for all intensive purposes equates to being smart. Management studies continually identify that the number one trait for successful managers to embody is the ability to be a good listener. However, the ability to increase your listening strength is different from your ability to have strong biceps. With lifting weights you see tangible reminders of your hard work. Increasing your listening ability takes similar repetitions and perseverance, but you don't have the visual results of your hard effort—although you will see improvements across your learning, speaking, and working endeavors. As a student you have many opportunities to sculpt your ability. The end result of this process is becoming a better student, spending less time studying, being a more desirable employee, and being a better friend and family member.

Listening is an active process involving both concentration and thinking. Sometimes there is a barrier that interferes with the listener's concentration. Following are eight barriers to concentration in listening.

Barriers to Listening

EXTERNAL NOISE External noise includes noises both inside and outside the listening area. Talking, footsteps, whispering, coughing, cell phones on vibrate, and street noise are some of the things that make it difficult to pay attention to a speaker. As a listener, you can avoid some distractions by arriving early enough at a lecture to get a seat where you can see and hear easily.

TAKE EFFECTIVE NOTES   Learning to take effective notes is an excellent way to improve your listening skills. Note taking promotes active listening and concentration. Rather than just listening passively to a speaker, the note taker must listen with the mind in order to identify the speaker's important ideas. It takes clear thinking and concentration to sort out main ideas from supporting details. Below are several note-taking tips.

1. *Write Down Only Important Ideas.* A good speech is planned around a central idea and several main points. The central idea is usually stated in the introduction of the speech. Sometimes a speaker will also list in the introduction the main points to be covered. Listen for signals that indicate that main ideas are forthcoming. Words like *specifically*, *further*, and *first* indicate that a speaker is moving from one point to another.

2. *Write Legibly.* Sometimes note takers write so hurriedly that when they finish, they can't read their own notes. If your notes are illegible, you are probably writing down too much.

3. *Keep Up.* If you find that you are falling behind in your note taking, skip a few lines and begin again. Later, when you expand your notes, you can fill in the missing information.

4. *Use Your Own Words.* One of the best ways to show that you understand something is to be able to explain it in your own words. When you translate the ideas of another into your own vocabulary, they will be easier to understand and remember.

5. *Be Brief.* A common mistake among inexperienced note takers is the tendency to write down too much. Don't try to write down everything the speaker says. A set of notes should be a summary of a speaker's main ideas.

6. *Don't Erase.* Rather than waste time erasing, draw a line through the mistake and continue. Remember, the notes you are taking are for your own use. If you want your notes to be neat, you can rewrite or type them later.

7. *Don't Worry about Spelling.* If you're not sure about how a word is spelled, write it phonetically. You can check the spelling later when you expand your notes.

8. *Date Your Notes.* Whether you are taking notes by hand or by computer, you should get into the habit of dating them with the day, month, and year. This will enable you to pinpoint a missed lecture or the specific date of a speech.

9. *Expand Your Notes.* If the notes you are taking are for the purpose of helping you remember information or to aid you in studying for an exam, it is wise to expand them as soon after a lecture as possible.

GETTING STARTED

If you are like most students, the thought of taking a speech course far from excites you. You most likely have some anxiety about standing up in front of a group of classmates to deliver a speech. You might be unclear as to how to develop a clear and interesting message. Possibly you are afraid you might forget what you planned to say in your speech, say the wrong thing, or say it ineffectively and be embarrassed. All the prior are legitimate concerns and this book and your course will allow you to overcome these fears. When all is said and done, you have much more on the line with a speaking orientated class than just a grade: You have the opportunity to create a more powerful, meaningful existence.

In today's global society, the person who can't communicate effectively is operating under a distinct handicap. People who are successful at the corporate level are invariably required to speak both within and outside the organization. Business and industrial employees are often required to take courses at the company's expense in order to improve their speech skills. Make no mistake, the ability to communicate effectively can often mean the difference between success and failure in the workplace.

People tend to equate the ability to speak well with the ability to think well. To a great extent, this is due to the fact that effective speakers are able to get their ideas across to others in an easy-to-understand, interesting way. Remember, every time you speak, you are communicating something about who you are to others. If you want others to see you as an effective communicator, two broad guidelines can help to ensure success: (1) say something worthwhile, and (2) say it in a confident, natural way.

Say Something Worthwhile

When you prepare a speech, you are concerned with two things: what you want to say and how you want to say it. What you say is called the *content* of your speech, which includes your subject, main idea and supporting material, organization, and the way you word your speech. Whenever you can, you should choose a worthwhile subject from your own area of interest so that you are familiar with what you are talking about and have some concern for your subject. Next, you must develop the subject with your audience in mind. An audience will pay attention to something that is either useful or interesting to them. If you can show your audience that your subject is useful to them, this will give them a reason to pay attention. Point out how your speech will be useful to your listeners in the introduction. If your subject is interesting to them, you can get their attention in the introduction and hold it throughout the speech.

If, however, your subject does not seem useful to your audience, is not interesting in itself, yet you still want to choose it because you feel it is worthwhile, in order to hold their attention you must make it interesting to them. Suggestions for getting and holding the attention of your audience are found in Chapter 2. Keep in mind that the less interesting or useful a subject is, the more difficult it will be to hold the audience's attention. For example, unless you were in a class of art students, an informative speech on Salvador Dali's contribution to modern art would take a lot more imagination and effort to make it interesting to a typical audience than a speech on the Beatle's influence on rock and roll.

Similarly, your listeners would be more likely to see the usefulness of a speech on the effects of alcohol on the mind and body than on one demonstrating how to make an arrow. Almost everyone takes a drink now and then or knows someone who does, perhaps taking more than he or she should. Knowing what the positives and negatives of drinking alcohol are would most likely seem useful to many. On the other hand, knowing how to make an arrow would probably only seem useful to a bow hunter or an avid archer.

This does not mean, however, that a speech demonstrating how to make an arrow could not be made interesting to a general audience. A number of years ago, one of my students, a Native American from a Wisconsin Chippewa tribe, delivered a speech on how to make an arrow. He brought in a modern apparatus for aligning the feathers and the arrowhead on the arrow shaft so that the arrow would be in perfect balance. He showed us a variety of modern arrows and bows. Then he showed us a number of bows and arrows that had been made by the members of his or other Ojibwa tribes over 150 years earlier. The arrowheads were flint, and the feathers had come from eagles or hawks. When he put the primitive arrows on the apparatus, they were way out of balance. The bows were obviously nowhere near as powerful as the ones made today. He explained that Indians wore moccasins and learned to walk without making a sound so that they could get close enough to hit whatever they were stalking with their primitive weapons. The speech was interesting and informative. It cleared up some misconceptions the class had from watching cowboy and Indian movies and gave the class a greater appreciation of the contributions and resourcefulness of Native Americans.

Say It in a Confident Way

The way you say something is called *delivery*. Delivery includes such things as eye contact, facial expression, body movement, personal appearance, and voice. Effective delivery should seem confident and natural. Besides an increase in volume for a larger audience, there are a number of differences between public speaking and ordinary conversation. First, public speaking is intentional. As the title of this text emphasizes, a speech is delivered with a clear purpose in mind. Second, a speech is more carefully prepared than everyday conversation. A subject is chosen and developed with a specific audience in mind, and words are chosen more carefully. If you want to deliver an effective speech, you must be clear about what you want to say and whom you are trying to reach. Remember, in most cases, the only interaction with your audience that you have in a speech situation is their nonverbal response.

Your delivery will seem more confident and natural if you use a conversational style. A conversational style makes frequent use of the personal experiences, which gives it an air of familiarity, as if the speaker were talking to close friends. Use your own vocabulary but eliminate words that might be considered overly casual or inappropriate. If you try to use words with which you are unfamiliar, your style will seem stilted and unnatural. You should, however, choose your words carefully. Keep in mind that speech is more formal than ordinary conversation, and your language should be a bit more formal too.

The advantage of using your own vocabulary when delivering a speech is that you will feel more natural and comfortable. Talking about something you feel is important and about which you are sincere will help you exude confidence.

At this point, you might be asking yourself, "How can I have confidence, when the thought of giving a speech gives my stomach butterflies?"

PROJECTING CONFIDENCE

Keep in mind that if you choose a topic from your own area of interest that you feel is worthwhile, prepare your speech carefully with a clear purpose and your audience in mind, and regularly practice your delivery beforehand, you will project confidence when delivering your speech. You might feel anxious (or nervous) before and during the speech, but unless you tell your audience that you are nervous, most likely they won't know.

For years I taught a course for business and professional people at a local university. The course was designed to improve speaking ability, particularly in the area of delivery. Most of the students who took that course were successful executive types with high-level jobs who were highly motivated to improve their ability to communicate effectively. The course met for 3 hr once a week, and at every class meeting, the whole class delivered a speech. After the speeches were delivered, the class discussed the presentations they had just experienced. The students soon discovered that although some felt nervous while delivering their speeches, this nervousness was not discernible to their audience. If someone said, "Boy, was I nervous," the response would invariably be, "You didn't look nervous." Once it became clear that their nervousness was not apparent to their classmates, the butterflies disappeared.

Another benefit of the course was that delivering a speech at every meeting gave each student important experience in speaking in front of a group. Since everyone was in the same boat, the group was highly supportive. The more speeches those students gave, the better they got. There is nothing like success to boost your confidence.

On the positive side, being a bit nervous before giving a speech is an indication that you are "keyed up," a desirable reaction. Have you ever watched a performer pace back and forth before going on stage or an athlete bending, stretching, or just moving around before competing? They are keyed up and they are letting off a bit of the nervous energy or excitement that is building up for that moment on stage, on the field, in the ring, or wherever they are going to perform. This energy works to their advantage, and it can work to yours, too, when you let it help you deliver an enthusiastic speech.

Energize Yourself

When you will be giving a speech in class, you won't be able to pace the floor, jump up and down, or do knee bends, but you can exercise isometrically, which should help you release some of your nervous energy. An isometric exercise is a procedure by which you contract a muscle for about 8 to 10 s against some immovable resistance, for example a chair, table, or floor. Here are some isometric exercises you can try:

1. While sitting on a chair with your feet flat on the floor, grasp each side of the chair and attempt to lift yourself.
2. Sit on a chair with your feet flat on the floor. Put your hands on top of your knees while drawing in your abdominal muscles. Attempt to lift your heels off the floor.
3. While sitting on a chair, place the palms of your hands on the sides of the chair and press inward as hard as you can with spread fingers.

A few minutes before it is your turn to speak, breathe in slowly and deeply through your nose until your lungs are full. Hold the breath for a count of four or five and slowly breathe out with jaw and lips relaxed, as if you are yawning. Repeat three or four times. Then, when it is your turn to speak, stand up and walk briskly and confidently up to the podium to deliver your speech.

The Truth about Nervousness

Nervousness is learned behavior. Stage fright is the fear that you will not do as well in front of an audience as you would like to. The symptoms of stage fright might be any of the following: rapid pulse, dry mouth, difficulty swallowing, trembling, sweaty palms, or queasy stomach. The phrase "butterflies in the stomach" is often used in regard to stage fright. Most people have no difficulty when communicating to others in small groups or in one-on-one situations; but, in larger groups this can often pose a problem.

Public speaking is probably the course feared by more students than any other. Why? Because many see the situation as threatening. They fear that others will be able to see their weaknesses and imperfections whether real or imaginary. Worrying too much, about what others will think about you is what causes stage fright, or to use a better term, speech fright.

This particular fear usually diminishes after the confidence-building sequence of easy speaking activities in the early part of the semester. The positive feedback from classmates and from your own instructor is very powerful, and when supplemented with positive self-talk, is very effective in replacing those fears from childhood. A more appropriate or rational nervousness is created because you care about what the audience thinks about you. This is especially true when you stand before a group of your peers. This concern for the opinion of your fellow human beings is appropriate if not carried too far. Appropriate caring causes you to do all you can to do your best. It gives you the extra rush of energy that you need to be really alive in front of an audience. Albert Ellis said in his book *A New Guide to Rational Living* that 98% of our anxiety is *overconcern* about what others will think of us. Overconcern is then the problem. Overconcern is usually stimulated and reinforced by negative self-talk such as, "I'm so nervous!", "I can't do this!", "I know I'll forget everything!", or that old classic self-fulfilling prophecy, "When I get in front of an audience my mind goes blank!" Say any of these affirmations enough and they tend to become the truth. Your strongest "word of honor" seems to be that spoken of yourself to yourself!

One really fascinating view of nervousness is that, on a physiological level, the physical signs of nervousness parallel the physical signs of excitement. That is to say that two people may experience the same symptoms and one may name it *nervousness* and the other may name it *excitement*. I urge every student to rename their nervous feelings sincerely as *excitement* and see how that changes their perception of their feelings.

For several semesters, I had students rank themselves as speakers and had the audience rank the speaker in terms of how nervous they were. I used a scale of 0 to 20. It was quite consistent that the speaker perceived himself to be twice as nervous as the audience would perceive him to be. That is, if a speaker said he was an 18 on the nervousness scale, the audience on the average would perceive him to be right close to 9 on that same scale. It is reassuring to realize that as a speaker a person only appears half as nervous to the audience as he thinks he appears.

HOW TO DEVELOP SELF-CONFIDENCE

As the oft-quoted saying "Nothing succeeds like success" implies, the experience of doing well in the speech activities in class will go a long way toward helping you develop greater self-confidence. To this end, always talk about something you really know, prepare, and practice very well. Be sincere and talk about things that really matter to you. Never ever try to "con" an audience into believing that you know something you do not. You cannot fool an audience. They can almost always tell exactly how much you do or do not know, how much time you have spent preparing, and above all how much time you spent rehearsing. Being well-prepared and well-rehearsed create almost certain success. This is what builds confidence.

Physically there are several very important things you can do to build self-confidence. First, be sure that you do not form the habit of holding your breath or breathing very shallowly. Many people, without even realizing it, breathe less deeply or even hold their breath when they experience stress. This can really backfire, as it can diminish the flow of oxygen to the brain, which may trigger a fear response that is mistaken for nervousness, not a physical reaction to lack of oxygen. Posture is also very important in developing self-confidence. If you stand with your weight evenly balanced on both feet, spine erect, head up, and arms loose at your side, your body will experience balance and comfort.

Psychologically there are several very important steps you can take to develop greater self-confidence. You can practice positive self-talk, repeatedly saying to yourself with as much conviction as you can create, "I can do this," "I can take it one step at a time," "I can become an excellent speaker," "This class is getting easier every week," and "I really want to learn to be a powerful speaker!" A second physiological exercise is to banish all talk of fear and nervousness. Substitute other less loaded words when you talk of your concerns. From now on, instead of "I'm really nervous," say "I'm really excited." If you are compelled to acknowledge your previous levels of nervousness, always say "In the past I have had some problems with nervousness, but it is getting better all of the time." Such relanguaging or renaming of something is a powerful way to gain control over your psychological reactions. Constantly using "I am very excited" and eliminating the fear and nervousness talk is a powerful technique for changing your whole response pattern to the public-speaking situation. In order for this to be effective in lessening nervousness, you do not have to believe strongly in your positive self-talk, but you *do* have to eliminate negative self-talk, or the positive and negative statements will cancel each other, leaving you to experience little growth in this area.

Another very powerful psychological idea is to change your focus from concern for yourself to concern for the audience. All too often a speaker is so focused on the impression he is making that he forgets to be really focused on how well the audience is hearing, seeing, understanding, and so forth. When your attention is turned back on yourself, your mind will be filled with questions like "Do I look scared?", "Do I sound stupid?", "What if I forget?", "Can they see my knees shaking?", and so on. The speaker who can forget himself and really be concerned whether the audience understands the very important ideas he is sharing will experience a genuine shift to a nurturing connection with the audience. This is the feeling that causes many a speaker to get "hooked" on public speaking. It is a very powerful feeling when you realize that you can share an idea that could change someone's life. This can only happen if you talk about things that are so very interesting and important to you that you truly want every person in the audience to understand. This means preparing well and working on that shift of focus. I have seen speakers experience this shift of focus, and when they had that experience, it eliminated most of their excessive nervousness.

Food Feeds Your Confidence

In addition to the pervious well-proven methods for increasing your confidence, it is important to heed the advice of the adage: "You are what you eat." Although drinking a Monster Energy Drink might seem like a good idea right before your speech, you are significantly altering your biology just by speaking in public, and it is best to limit the other variables interacting in your ecosystem. During normal daily life, the result of drinking something sugar filled or caffeinated might be positive, but excess sugar or caffeine, coupled with some stress, often play havoc on the body of the speaker. There has also been a recent movement in America to reduce or eliminate the consumption of wheat for many people. This diet, called gluten free, has been proven to help a growing segment of people to reduce cloudy thinking, excessive nervousness as well as many other physical ailments.

Stretch Your Comfort Zone

Your comfort zone is defined by your self-concept, your family culture, your community and national culture, and so on. As long as you are not violating any of the "rules" of any of these belief systems, you are in your comfort zone.

Some of these rules are appropriate but many are just habits handed down which end up creating a big rut that controls the direction of our life more than most of us realize. A more general approach to building confidence is to look constantly for opportunities to stretch your comfort zone in every area of life. If you are more comfortable waiting for someone else to speak first, push yourself to speak first as often as possible. Be on the lookout for little ways you can stretch that comfort zone. Push yourself in class. Keep more questions in store. Ask for information. Try dressing differently. Seek leadership roles. Volunteer some time at the library literacy program. Go to a town council meeting and ask a question. Take voice lessons. Take flying lessons. Go horseback riding. Drive somewhere you have never been. Challenge yourself to be aware and to act by choice, not by habit. Try out for a role in a community theater play.

Visual Imagery Is a Powerful Tool

The next delivery topic is a visual imagery technique specifically for developing confidence in public speaking. Mental rehearsal is another name for visual imagery. This technique is a fascinating tool for changing behavior, and the same procedure presented on the next few pages can be adapted to create behavior change in any area of life. You could even use it to practice remembering more and scoring better on the quizzes and to stop procrastinating and do that paperwork and other preparations early. Be creative and see how many areas you can find to try the three-step method of visual imagery you are now going to learn.

VISUAL IMAGERY FOR CONFIDENCE IN PUBLIC SPEAKING

Visual imagery for behavior change is a powerful technique. The legendary tennis coach Vic Braden was known for his quote "Learn to think like a winner—think positive and visualize your strengths." Braden took this idea to the courts as he statistically counted how many first serves his students would get into the service box by just serving the ball without any prior thinking. Then he coached his students to visualize, in their minds, their serve hit perfect and going into the service box. After visualizing the serve, the students had a significant improved percentage of actual serves that would go into the service box.

The subconscious mind does not seem to differentiate between actual physical rehearsal and mental rehearsal (visual imagery) when the mental rehearsal is done with the same concentration and vivid feelings associated with the actual physical rehearsal. The benefits from mental rehearsal done well are many. The rehearsal is completely under the control of the person doing the imagery; therefore, each rehearsal can be a positive, strengthening experience. The time involved is much less than actual practice requires, therefore more practice can be done. The troublesome spots in an activity can be repeatedly practiced easily. The subconscious mind can build a storehouse of "success" feelings about an activity. These feelings then encourage continued successful performance just as actual successful rehearsal would.

The visual imagery pattern I recommend for speech students desiring to experience more confidence and greater speaking skill in front of an audience is a simple three-step pattern. It is suggested that you practice using this pattern (or your own personal version of it) at least three times a day. Each session should be brief (2 to 5 min) but as intensely vivid and "real" as you can create it. Do this brief visual imagery three or more times a day for 2 to 3 weeks or longer and you will find a tremendous development of skill and confidence as the result. Each session should take only 2 to 3 min. Visual imagery can be done in any place where you can be uninterrupted for a few minutes. The very best schedule is morning, midday, and evening. Detailed instructions for using the visual imagery pattern follow.

A SCRIPT FOR USING VISUAL IMAGERY TO DEVELOP CONFIDENCE IN SPEAKING

Step One: Systematic Relaxation

Pay particular attention to shoulders, face, and stomach muscles. The purpose of step one is to focus attention away from your outer environment onto your physical body, then relax your body sufficiently to avoid it becoming a distraction later in the process when you focus your attention within yourself. Sit in a centered posture—do not recline. Start with your toes and systematically relax every part of your body up to the very top of your head. Tensing and relaxing is good if at first your shoulders or other large muscle groups are very tense.

Step Two: Favorite Peaceful Place

Picture a vivid sensory-rich scene in nature. You should use this same scene over and over or at least until you change projects. I usually use the beach. Focus on all the sensory details possible—sky, water, waves, sunlight, sun's warmth, sounds of birds and water, feel of sand underfoot, and so on. See yourself walking along the beach experiencing the colors, sights, sounds, touches, and freedom of the beach as vividly as you can.

Step Three: Rehearsing Your Desired Behavior

Picture yourself doing the behavior you desire to do just as perfectly as you hope to learn to do it—speaking with confidence and skill. The sequence I recommend is to see yourself sitting at your desk, aware that you are the next speaker. When it is your turn, you rise confidently and walk to the podium. You look confidently at individuals in the audience, and then begin with a ringing powerful opening statement. See yourself standing and speaking with real authority and clarity. You do not have to "hear" any actual words. Feel the energy and enthusiasm in your delivery. See people in the audience nodding their heads in agreement with your ideas. Feel your strong desire to communicate the interest and the importance of the information you are sharing. See yourself finishing with a strong dynamic ending statement. Hear the loud spontaneous applause as your audience acknowledges your excellent speech. Notice how you really enjoy the feeling of having done a good job. Feel this enjoyment. This is a very important ingredient in the visualization—your enjoyment of your success. See yourself now returning to your seat with the same sincere and confident attitude. See yourself sitting with a big smile on your face—very pleased with yourself. Enjoy and strengthen this feeling for a few moments before you open your eyes and are finished with the session.

ETHICS IN COMMUNICATION

Ethics in communication requires honesty. It requires a communicator to give only truthful and accurate information to an audience. This is an important responsibility and one not to be taken lightly.

Unfortunately, there are those in our society who believe in getting by any way they can. Too many political candidates offer us whatever it takes to ensure their election. We get daily accounts of those in government and business who have violated our trust in order to further their own causes. Too many advertisers justify their sales pitches with the slogan *caveat emptor* (let the buyer beware).

We are constantly bombarded with TV and radio commercials that promise us instant satisfaction if only we buy the advertised product. "Brush with our brand of toothpaste" or "buy our hair spray and shampoo"—these ads tell us and we will be successful, approved of, popular, or whatever we desire. And, too often, even though we realize that what we are receiving is often fabrication and misrepresentation, we just shake our heads and do nothing but regret that we can't trust many of the advertisers, politicians, elected officials, and others who have a direct influence on our lives. That is unfortunate because as receivers of messages we have the right to demand that those who communicate to us provide us with honest and accurate information.

Most of the ethical decisions that we make in our lives are based on our moral standards and values. Our decisions to respect the rights of others, to treat others with dignity, and to be true to our word are all ethical choices we make based on the value system to which we ascribe.

As a speaker, you have an ethical responsibility to your listeners to give them the same kind of honest and accurate information you would want them to give you. Document the statistics you use in your speech. Avoid using vague phrases such as "recent studies indicate" or "the latest surveys show." Instead, indicate exactly when and by whom the statistics you are stating were compiled. This will increase your credibility in the minds of your listeners. Chances are that some in your audience have been misled in the past by statistics. Pointing out exactly where your statistics came from and who compiled them will make the statistics you are using both reputable and unbiased and will set your audience's minds at ease.

When you back up your statements with the testimony of others, make sure you choose experts whom your audience will consider well qualified and objective. If the experts are unknown to your audience, give information about them that will establish their qualifications and objectivity.

Be especially careful when citing information you have gotten from the Internet. Wikipedia is not a quality source to cite in a speech. It is a good idea to save the material you are citing so that you can compare it to other sources you are using. When evaluating information you find on the Internet, make sure the material is current, objective, and reputable. The better the reputation of the author or the reliability of the sponsoring organization, the more likely it will be that the information is accurate.

Always make sure that your purpose is absolutely clear to the audience. For example, if your purpose is to persuade your audience to vote against establishing the death penalty in their state, let them know early on that that is what you are asking them to do. In the interest of fairness, it is also wise to present some of the arguments from the other side. This will demonstrate to your audience that you are interested in their reaching a well-informed decision. Furthermore, it will enable you to point out some of the weaknesses in the opposing viewpoint as well.

Whenever you use the ideas of others, you must give them credit. Even if you put their opinions or assertions in your own words by paraphrasing them rather than quoting them verbatim, you have a responsibility to acknowledge the source of information that is not your own. Presenting their words or ideas without giving them credit is *plagiarism*. Plagiarism can involve either presenting the ideas of others' word for word as they were written or spoken or paraphrasing the ideas in your own words. It makes no difference. Whenever you use the ideas of others without giving them credit, you are stealing from them. It doesn't matter whether you do this intentionally or through carelessness; it is stealing nonetheless. In the context of public speaking, plagiarism shouldn't exist because in nearly every case you will sound more qualified if you reference someone else as stating the information rather than you misleading the audience as if the words were your own.

Sometimes you may engage in plagiarism without intending to or even being aware of it. Suppose, for example, that you are a member of a group opposed to the manufacturing and sale of land mines in the United States. Because you have attended many meetings and are preoccupied with the issue, you have accumulated a substantial amount of material on this topic. Certainly some of the information from fliers and other handouts could have been taken from unidentified sources. Some of the ideas that you now embrace as your own could have come from others. Presenting them without giving credit to these sources would make you guilty of plagiarism. You can protect yourself by indicating to your audience that some of your ideas have come from the anti-land-mine organization of which you are a member. An added benefit will be that indicating your membership in the organization will also increase your credibility.

Make no mistake, plagiarism is the presenting of someone's words and ideas as if they were your own whether intentional or not, and the penalties for plagiarism at many schools are often severe, ranging from a failing grade on the assignment to failing the course or even being expelled from school. Some of the synonyms for plagiarize listed in *Roget's Thesaurus* are counterfeit, filch, lift, pinch, pirate, sneak, steal, and swipe.

Those who are caught plagiarizing outside the school often suffer significant penalties as well. Careers have been ruined, promotions denied, elections lost, and reputations irreparably damaged all because someone used the words or ideas of others in spoken or written communication, without giving the originator of those words or ideas credit.

Obviously then, you must be careful to take comprehensive notes that include the name of the author, the title, where you found the information, and date of publication when gathering information for your speech. If you are quoting the material exactly, use quotation marks and make sure of the word order and punctuation. If you are paraphrasing, make sure you capture the author's meaning. It is also a great idea if you cut and paste information from an online source to instantly change the color of the text you paste into your document as well as put where you found the information in parenthesis. The change of color will keep it obvious that the words were in fact taken from another source and were never created by you.

An ethical speaker avoids exaggeration and distortion. While we expect our friends to increase the size of the deer they shot or the length of the fish they caught when telling us about it, overstating the facts in a speech is unacceptable. Your audience deserves honest and accurate information. Equally unacceptable is distortion or misrepresentation of the facts. Unfortunately, one of my former students learned this the hard way. In delivering a speech on the evil of drinking and driving, she told the audience in graphic detail how her brother, his wife, and two little children had been killed by a drunken driver in an auto accident a few months earlier. The speech was very moving and many in the audience had tears in their eyes. As the class was leaving, someone asked her how the rest of the family was holding up under the strain and she said she had made the story up to make the speech more effective. As a result of this misrepresentation, her reputation in the class was damaged and she suffered a loss of credibility for the rest of the semester. What it all boils down to is this. An ethical speaker has a responsibility to present accurate and honest information that is free from exaggeration, distortion, or bias.

An ethical speaker must be tolerant of others. The strength of our world lies in its diversity. People will always have differing viewpoints, beliefs, and values, but an ethical speaker has a responsibility to respect the variety of individuals that comprise the globe. The use of biased language or unkind references to others because of their race, ethnic background, religion, sexual orientation, or viewpoints is unacceptable. As an ethical speaker you must be willing to listen to views that are different from your own. And in a global world, we must all realize that we are going to be dealing with a large group of society that doesn't share our same background.

Finally, what an audience thinks of you has a definite effect on their reaction to what you are saying to them. If they see you as being ethical, friendly, and competent, they will respond to you in a receptive and friendly manner. What is even more important is that you see yourself as being ethical, friendly, and competent. The more accurate a picture you have of yourself and your self-worth, the more likely it will be that you will communicate ethically, accurately, and successfully.

DISCUSSION QUESTIONS

1. Describe some communication breakdowns that you have experienced and identify the causes. What could you have done to improve the situation?
2. Why do you think visualization helps our speaking ability?
3. Can you describe how you feel when you have butterflies in your stomach?

EXERCISES

1. List some similarities between public speaking and answering questions at a job interview?
2. List five ways technology has changed public speaking?
3. In a group, discuss how the Internet has made public speaking more or less powerful for society? Describe your view.

2 Audience Analysis

After you have selected a subject and determined your purpose, you are ready to think of your speech in terms of your audience. An audience is an indispensable part of communication. If your audience fails to understand or pay attention to your message, communication does not take place. Therefore, when you develop your speech, do so with your audience in mind.

It can be a difficult task keeping our audience in sight. The groups we are often normally acquainted with such as our neighbors, church groups, friends, coworkers are different than a general audience. In other words, the larger audience who you will be speaking to is not as similar to you as most of your other personal groups. A well-versed and educated speaker knows how to address the larger, more varied audience and how to get them to be interested and enthused about what she has to say.

WHO EXACTLY IS MY AUDIENCE?

As you prepare the content of your speech, consider who is in your audience. Your boss or teacher? Your coworkers or classmates? Try to put yourself into their shoes. Think how they may think. Even if there is only one male or one female in an otherwise all-female or all-male audience, you must consider this person when preparing your speech. A surprising number of communications fail because the speaker has been unclear as to the composition of his or her audience. Take the case of George Scott, assistant cashier of a small Midwestern bank. George came home in a state of dejection one night after having been passed over for promotion for the third time. He called his sister-in-law Phyllis, a close friend of the bank president's wife, and asked her to try to find out why. She learned the following: George considered himself a great storyteller and was particularly fond of ethnic jokes. He often told these jokes, both at the office and at holiday and other office get-togethers. What George failed to realize was that a number of people, including the bank president, found this sort of humor at the expense of others patently offensive. Whenever an opportunity for advancement occurred, George was rejected as being too insensitive. He paid a high price for not knowing his audience.

As you listen to your classmates, speeches and talk with them, keep in mind that they are your audience for this course. It may help to make note of their interests, consider their backgrounds, knowledge, and attitudes toward your subject and then develop your speech accordingly. A good speaker may want to occasionally tie in examples that may be directed at other presentations or class member interests in the course. This personal touch helps to show that the speaker was also paying attention as a listener, and it can increase the audience's opinion of the speaker.

WHAT RESPONSE CAN I REASONABLY EXPECT FROM MY AUDIENCE?

No matter how good a speech looks on paper or how well it is delivered, its success or failure must always be measured in terms of audience response. A salesperson who doesn't sell the product will soon be out of a job, the comedienne who doesn't evoke laughter will fall flat on her face, and the politician who doesn't get votes will not get elected. Therefore, when developing your speech, you must always consider whether the response you are seeking is realistic.

When the president of the United States is going to give a speech, the White House staff look into the location, who will attend, how many will attend, etc. They do this foreshadowing of the event so the president and his aides know exactly who the audience will be. The president will alter his speech to adapt to the audiences (different word choices and examples for Wall Street bankers vs. soybean farmers). In addition to adapting the presentation itself, the president will also adapt his attire. He will know beforehand if he is required to be in formal attire—or if perhaps he is meeting with union auto workers and he will take a more casual approach with his shirt cuffed up to his elbows. This process helps the president to adapt to the audience both with his messages as well as his physical appearance.

Regardless of how well you know your audience makeup, some responses might be unattainable. Your audience might not have the background or experience necessary for you to be able to teach them how to repair a computer or sew a dress. A lack of time or resources might prevent you from showing your audience how to tile a floor or write the computer code for a computer game.

WILL MY AUDIENCE FIND THIS SUBJECT USEFUL?

People willingly pay attention if they will gain something from doing so. You pay attention to the directions for filling out your income-tax forms because you have something to gain if you do—and something to lose if you don't.

You listen to a dull story told by your boss or prospective in-law and laugh because it is in your best interest to do so.

If for some reason members of your audience *need* to know the information you will be giving them in your speech, tell them they do. If they will prevent the possible costly repair to their cars by engaging in a do-it-yourself car maintenance program, if they have a responsibility to act against the growing problem of child abuse, or if they might possibly save a life by taking a Red Cross CPR course, let them know at the beginning of the speech. To show an audience how to react to an accident at home and then explain to them only at the conclusion of your speech that the majority of accidents occur at home would be to leave a number of those in your audience thinking, "I guess I should have listened."

I recently had a speech in my course that was directed toward getting everyone out of debt in 5 years. The speaker, Dennis, told the class at the beginning the importance of heeding his advice. For the next 7 min he detailed the best ways of attacking credit card debt as well as reducing unnecessary expenses. There was not one class member who was not fixated on the information—and for one reason: it was useful to the audience.

WILL MY AUDIENCE FIND THIS SUBJECT INTERESTING?

The second reason that people pay attention is to satisfy an interest. Less effort is required to pay attention to what is interesting than to what is useful. Consider your own experience. Have you ever watched an unimaginative educational film because you knew there would be an exam about it? Have you listened to an uninteresting lecture because you knew it would have an effect on your grade? How much did you learn in that course? How much do you remember? In both cases, you had, in effect, something to gain by paying attention. Did it pay off? Now compare the uninteresting educational film or the lecture to the educational TV program *Sesame Street*. It is estimated that *Sesame Street* has a viewing audience of 10 million. The people who write and produce the program handle their material in such an interesting way that paying attention (and thus learning) is no longer a chore—it is fun. Your job as a speaker is to develop your material interestingly. While you can do this with someone you know quite well, how can you do it with strangers?

If you are familiar with the subject you have chosen, you should be able to make an educated guess. Suppose you choose to speak about one of your two hobbies, raising tropical fish or restoring antique cars. The majority of your friends have shown more interest in your antique cars than in your fish. Some might have even changed the subject when you asked if they wanted to see your baby swordtails. Probably, a general audience would have greater initial interest in antique cars. This, however, does not mean you could not choose to speak about raising tropical fish. You can do it effectively if you build your audience's interest to gain and maintain their attention. You might begin by introducing your listeners to the piranha, one of the most interesting fish you own. A description of this voracious, sometimes man-eating, creature as even more dangerous than the great white shark is a surefire attention-getter.

A good current example of keeping public speaking interesting is Sir Ken Robinson's TED.com presentation. TED.com is an online streaming video service showing 18 min lectures by some of the world's brightest thinkers. Having that much IQ on the stage, one might guess it would be dull or stagnate but the speeches on the site are just the opposite. These speakers have realized the importance of keeping their material interesting and engaging (while delivering the important messages). I urge you to peruse TED.com to let presentation styles speak for themselves.

WHAT IS MY AUDIENCE'S KNOWLEDGE OF MY SUBJECT?

Considering what your listeners already know about your subject is an important part of audience analysis. A too technical approach could leave them thoroughly confused; repeating what they already know is sure to bore them.

If your audience has little or no knowledge of your subject, you must explain unfamiliar terminology and concepts to them. Keep in mind that this lack of knowledge will have an effect on their ability to respond. You could not expect those in your audience who have little idea of what is under the hood of a car to learn how to "tune-up" a car after your speech. Nor could a nonsewer be expected to know how to install a zipper or cuff a pair of pants after a presentation. Your educated guess as to the audience's knowledge of your subject should be an important consideration in terms of your choice of subject and purpose for each speech you make.

WHAT DEMOGRAPHIC CHARACTERISTICS SHOULD I CONSIDER ABOUT MY AUDIENCE?

The word *demography* is derived from the Greek word *demos*, meaning "people." The demographic consideration of your audience has to do with their vital statistics: age, education, beliefs, income, special interests, and so on. These characteristics can often help you in determining how to handle your subject. For example, as a rule, young people tend to be more physically active than older people, more inclined to engage in sports rather than watch them. Consequently, when talking about a particular sport, you might treat it as a participation sport for a younger audience and as a spectator sport for an older group.

The educational level of your audience could be important to you for a number of reasons. One of these has to do with the relationship between education and vocabulary. You must speak to an audience in familiar words that they can understand instantly. For example, you wouldn't explain the process of osmosis to your 11-year-old sister in the same way you'd explain it to your college speech class. Another consideration is that a well-educated audience will be more aware of vital issues and current events than a less educated one will.

How many members of your audience come from different cultures? Never before in our history has the ethnic, cultural, and racial population in our country been so diverse. Each of us belongs to a variety of groups that have a distinct effect on the way we communicate. As indicated in Chapter 1, communication breakdowns occur even when communicating with those who are members of the groups to which we belong. Even more common are communication breakdowns between people from different cultures and subcultures. In analyzing your audience, try to consider any cultural characteristic, attitude, or sentiment that might bear on your speech topic.

Do those in your audience have similar attitudes and beliefs? Do they have special interests in common? Are they rich or poor, Republican or Democrat, conservative or liberal? Any of these demographic characteristics might be important to you as you prepare your speech.

Outside of the speech class, demographic information is equally important. If you remember you at one time signed up for a grocery store "plus card," which allowed you to receive in store coupons for your purchases. What you most likely have forgotten is the process that transpired for you to get the card. You were required to fill out a specific form: the questions asked your age, address, sex, ethnicity, relationship status, salary. All demographic traits were on the form. After giving the store the data, they now are able to track all of your purchases, forever, and relate those sales to your demographic data via the swipe or scan of your "plus card." This information comes with a hefty price tag attached as the retailers sell this data to companies wanting to advertise products. When the advertisers purchase this data, they learn that their product relates best to women aged 34 to 50 who make $35,000 a year and live in a certain city.

Just like the retailers coveting the demographic data, remember, the success of your speech is equally determined in terms of reaching your audience. Did your audience get the information you wanted them to have? Were they entertained? Did you get them to take the action you wanted? The more you know about your audience, the more likely it will be that you will achieve your purpose.

IS MY AUDIENCE'S ATTITUDE FAVORABLE, INDIFFERENT, OR OPPOSED?

A Favorable Audience

Perhaps the greatest advantage to dealing with a favorable audience is that they are usually both supportive and attentive. Your goal when communicating to them is to reinforce their positive attitudes. If they enjoy humor, the more effectively you entertain them with your humor, the more successful you will be. If they would benefit from some tips on simple car maintenance, their satisfaction will be measured by how clearly you can explain your directions. The more effectively you can reinforce their positive attitudes, the more likely you will be able to move them to action.

An Indifferent Audience

When you feel that many in your audience will be indifferent to your sub-ject, your job is to stimulate their interest. Make it clear to the audience why they should listen to your speech. You might point out why the sub-ject is useful to them and how they will gain something from listening, you might give them information that will trigger their curiosity or interest, or you might point out how the problem affects them and why they need to listen to your plan for solving the problem. In each case, the action must be taken early in your introduction in order to gain the attention of your audience and hold it.

A successful speech to an indifferent audience was given by Erik Jackson, a second-year photography student. From conversations he had with them, Erik was aware that many of his classmates did not share his interest in photography and did not own expensive cameras or equipment. So, rather than delivering a complicated speech involving f-stops or light meters, Erik decided to give his speech class information about photog-raphy that would be useful to them no matter what kind of equipment they had.

Erik began his speech by showing those in his audience several pages of pictures from a photo album. He had enlarged each of the pictures so that they could easily be seen, even by those in the back of the room. He called his classmates' attention to the fact that other than there being different people in each, the photos were very much alike. In each snapshot, people stood rigidly together in a line with smiles on their faces.

Next Erik showed the class a few variations of the first pictures he had shown. Although the people in them were the same, these snapshots were much more interesting than the first set. In some, the arrangement of people was much more imaginative. In others, the background made the group stand out much more vividly. By explaining about camera angle, posing, and pic-ture balance, Erik demonstrated to his audience that with a little imagination they could take pictures that were more interesting.

An Opposed Audience

Perhaps the hardest audience to deal with is one that is opposed to your point of view or dislikes your subject. Who hasn't spent hours arguing about reli-gion or politics only to wind up even more convinced than ever that he was right and the other fellow wrong? It is difficult to convince a person to change a point of view or opinion that may have taken her years to form. By the time a person reaches adulthood, many of his attitudes are pretty well fixed. Stud-ies indicate that there is little change in viewpoint among those who listen to or read things with which they strongly disagree.

Fortunately, occasions are rare when a speaker or writer must address an audience opposed to her subject or viewpoint. It is difficult, for example, to imagine a pro-choice article in the *Catholic Herald Citizen* or to picture

Elton John delivering a speech on same-sex marriages at a Republican National Convention.

Mary Smith, a junior college freshman, used a common-ground approach in preparing a speech to inform on one of her favorite subjects, opera. She had found that most of her classmates were apathetic or even hostile to her subject. One fellow named Ron intended to cut class on the day of her speech because opera, especially Wagnerian opera, Mary's favorite, really "turned him off."

On the day she delivered her speech, Mary identified with many in her audience by beginning:

> You know, like many of you I was really turned off by opera until 2 years ago, when I found out an interesting fact. I didn't like opera because I didn't know anything about it. Well, ever since then the more I got to know about it, the more I got to like it. I'm sure when you get to know enough about it, you'll like it too.

Mary realized that she needed a fresh, imaginative approach to hold the attention of her audience. She prepared carefully and thoughtfully, and delivered to the class a humorous plot summary of Wagner's opera *Tannhauser*, which ended to even Ron's delight with the heroine getting stabbed right between the two big trees.

Mary took what many in her audience thought was a dull, boring topic and made it exciting and interesting. She used humor, novelty, conflict, and suspense to hold their attention, and the result was a successful speech.*

LISTENING NEEDS

In addition to understanding the importance of taking the audiences, diverse views into account, it is equally important to realize that all listeners, and people, share a general system of needs. For the speaker, it is important to understand these needs because by directing emphasis at them is an effective way to make our speech pertinent for all listeners. Physical well-being, safety and security, love and belonging, esteem, and self-actualization are all vital in what the psychologist Abraham H. Maslow described as the Hierarchy of Needs.

Maslow details that some of the needs are more important than others and have to be met before an individual can climb higher up toward the top. For instance, if you are in an airplane which suddenly loses oxygen, you will not think about anything until you have the yellow plastic cup around your face.

---

*Materials on pages 32 to 35 used with permission from Arthur Koch and Stanley B. Felber, *What Did You Say?*, 3rd ed. (Upper Saddle River, NJ: Prentice-Hall, 1985).

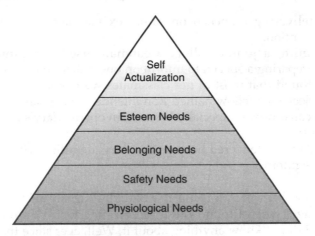

Maslow's Hierarchy of Needs

The base level of need that Maslow details is represented as physiological needs. *Physiological needs* are enough air to breathe, water to drink, and food to eat. These needs are the base since they support the realization of all the following needs. If these needs are not met, the individual will continue to seek out these items and forego climbing up the progression.

If the listener has enough food to eat, water to drink, and air to breathe, then they progress to becoming concerned with safety needs. *Safety needs* represent that we all need a secure and safe personal world. We don't want to feel threatened or have the possibility being physically hurt. This concern is only realized if we have food, air, and water.

If the listener has enough food to eat, water to drink, and air to breathe and they are not in an environment that will hurt them, they progress to Maslow's third level: *belonging need*. This is the need to be loved and respected by those closest to us. The love we receive from our parents, our boyfriend or girlfriend, or our husband or wife is a critical human need.

If the listener has love, in addition to safety and the base physiological needs, they progress to the esteem needs. *Esteem needs* represent individuals feeling they have some worth and importance in their life. This stage represents individuals beginning to take pride in themselves and their thoughts. People like to feel in charge, in control of their destiny, and not dictated by the constraints of others.

And finally, if you have enough air to breathe, water to drink, and food to eat, are safe, and find yourself loved by people around you and start to develop some personal pride, then you progress to the top level. *Self-actualization* is when individuals begin to make the most out of themselves and their abilities. It is here that the confidence is developed to go against the grain and become a unique, pioneering spirit. Of course, all individuals have different visions of what they want to achieve. Regardless of the end destination, self-actualization allows us to be good at our specialization.

It is vital that we, as speakers, keep the audience, their interests and their needs at our forefront of thought. After all, it is the audience that is allowing us the honor and privilege to speak by sitting quietly. Let's think of your audience in terms of capitalistic salary for a moment. Let's hypothetically say each member of your class is a $50,000-a-year employee. If there are 25 students in your class, you will be speaking to an audience that equates to a $1,250,000 salary. Wouldn't you try heavily to impress that level of leader? You have the floor, and their attention. Use it wisely.

AUDIENCE ANALYSIS FORM

Name _____ Date _____

Title of Speech _____

(Answer each question completely.)

THE COMMUNICATOR

1. Why have I chosen this subject?

2. What qualifies me to deal with this subject?

THE MESSAGE

3. What is my specific purpose?

4. What response can I reasonably expect?

THE AUDIENCE

5. Will my audience find this subject interesting?

6. Will my audience find this subject useful?

7. What is the audience's probable knowledge of my subject?

8. What characteristics of my audience should I consider in preparing my subject?

FIGURE 2.1 Audience Analysis Form

AUDIENCE ANALYSIS EVALUATION FORM

Name _____

1. What was the communicator's subject?

2. How interesting was this subject to you?

| | | | | |
low   high

3. How useful was this subject to you?

| | | | | |
low   high

4. How effectively did the communicator get attention during introduction?

| | | | | |
low   high

5. How much preparation was put into this communication?

| | | | | |
low   high

6. What was the communicator's specific purpose? (one simple, declarative sentence)

| | | | | |
low   high

7. How effective was the conclusion to the communication?

| | | | | |
low   high

8. How well did the communicator accomplish his purpose?

| | | | | |
low   high

COMMENTS:

FIGURE 2.2 Audience Analysis Evaluation Form

DISCUSSION QUESTIONS

1. Why is the audience important in public speaking?
2. As a speaker how do we get information on our audience?
3. What are some topics that you think might be of interest to the class?

EXERCISES

1. Prepare a list of topics that would be interesting to your audience.
2. Select a topic like "Is global warming occurring?", "Do you like Oprah Winfrey?", "Do you like Eminem?", or "Are electric cars a good value?" Make one wall of your classroom the "yes" wall, and the other the "no" wall. After reading each topic, have your class situate themselves somewhere between the walls based on how much they agree or disagree with the topic. Look around and notice how many people have differing opinions to you.
3. The audience analysis form (Figure 2.1) and the audience analysis evaluation form (Figure 2.2) are designed to aid you in better understanding your audience. Fill out a copy of the audience analysis form during the planning of your speech. Many of the answers you put down on the form will be educated guesses about your audience.

3 Determine Your Purpose and Subject

In order to develop an effective speech, you must have a clear purpose in mind. The title of this book, *Speaking with a Purpose*, emphasizes the importance of purpose in communication. Your goal as a speaker should be to achieve a desired response from your audience. Beginning speakers often fail because they pay too little attention to purpose of their speech and specifically hone in the audience response they want to attain. The following are the major purposes in speaking:

1. *To Entertain* to elicit a pleasurable response, to provoke curiosity, to provide suspense, or to amuse. Treating a serious subject lightly or a light subject seriously and describing an unusual or exciting experience are examples of communication to entertain.
2. *To Inform* to add to the knowledge or understanding of the listener. Demonstrating how to do something, explaining a process, reporting on a meeting, and describing an event are examples of communication to inform.
3. *To Persuade* to convince, to reinforce, or to activate. Since persuasion is the most complex and powerful form of speaking, the three types of persuasion will be treated separately.
   a. *To Convince*—to change your listener's opinions or to commit them to a point of view about which they are undecided. Persuasion to convince occurs frequently in debate and in problem-solving discussion. In both, information is given to listeners in an attempt to get them to change their minds or to form an opinion on something about which they are undecided. Persuasion to convince relies heavily on a logical approach using reasoning, statistics, testimony, comparison, and factual examples.

b. *To Reinforce*—to arouse and invigorate an audience already in agreement with the speaker's point of view. A speech at a pep rally in the school auditorium before a football or basketball game is a good example of persuasion to reinforce. The students do not have to be convinced about the importance of their team's winning. The idea is to strengthen their attitude about winning, to build a fire under them so that they are prepared emotionally and enthusiastically for the game. Persuasion to reinforce largely employs a psychological approach—appealing to the attitudes, beliefs, sentiments, and motives of the audience.

c. *To Activate*—to put into action. In the previous example, the speaker's job is to stimulate the members of the student audience to become even more excited than they already are about the upcoming game. However, they are not given specific instructions as to what to do in terms of that excitement. In persuasion to activate, the audience should be told exactly what action you want to be accomplished. A speech by the coach to the team in the locker room before the game is a good example of persuasion to activate. The team is told specifically to go out and "win one for the alma mater." The speech to activate asks the audience to buy, to sell, to join, to march, or the like. While it can employ persuasion to convince or to reinforce or both, it is by far more successful when directed to an audience who has already agreed. Obviously, if you want to get your audience to do something, you are bound to be more successful if it is already predisposed to act that way.

SELECTING A SUBJECT

Once you clearly understand the general purpose of your speech, you are ready to choose a subject. There will undoubtedly be times when you will be asked to deliver a speech on a topic that has already been determined. For example, you are asked to give a report on a convention you attended for your employer. Or as a member of the student government, you are assigned to speak on one aspect of tuition increases. In a different situation, the occasion might determine what your subject will be. However, more often than not, you will need to select your own subject.

You may be fortunate and have a topic quickly emerge that you have interest in and which you feel will be interesting to your audience. If this happens, you can immediately begin developing your speech. However, if you can't think of an appropriate subject, take out a sheet of paper and write down as many things as you can that you are interested in or have experience with. There is no better place to look for a subject than in your own background. Did you grow up on a farm? Did you come from a different part of the country? Where have you traveled? Do you have special skills in athletics, music, graphic arts, theater, or fashion design? What hobbies do you have? What are your political views? What issues interest you? What do you talk about with close friends? With some imagination and hard work, you can make these subjects interesting to your audience. When determining which subject to choose, ask yourself the following questions:

1. Is the subject suited to my purpose?
2. Is the subject interesting to me?
3. Am I qualified to speak on this subject?
4. Will my audience find this subject interesting?
5. Will my audience find this subject useful?
6. Is my subject sufficiently narrowed?

Is the Subject Suited to My Purpose?

Suppose you are asked to deliver a speech whose general purpose is to inform. Because you have recently begun studying the U.S. Army School of the Americas in your Latin America history class, you decide to deliver an informative speech about this school, which was established in 1946 at Fort Benning, Georgia. As you begin developing the speech and find out more about the school, however, you learn that during the last 50 years, the School of the Americas has trained more than 87,000 Latin American and Caribbean soldiers, many of whom have committed some of the worst human rights violations in our hemisphere, and that officers who studied at the school are responsible for the torture, killing, and maiming of hundreds of thousands of innocent people in Latin America and that many graduates have destabilized democratic institutions or overthrown their governments. This would most likely give your listeners a highly negative view of this school, which one Central American newspaper dubbed "School of the Assassins." This subject would be better suited as a speech with the general purpose to persuade and the specific purpose to activate your audience to write their representative in Congress to support the Kennedy Bill, HR 2652, which will cut off funding for the School for the Americas, effectively closing it down.

Is the Subject Interesting to Me?

Whenever possible, choose a subject you find interesting. Enthusiasm and passion are key factors to successful speaking. If you talk enthusiastically about something, this enthusiasm is bound to rub off on your audience. If you are passionate and invested in a topic, your audience will have more interest in your message and is more likely to retain the information. Are you excited about a particular kind of music or art form? Are you into alternative rock or ballet? Do you jog or lift weights? Collect coins? With a little imagination and some effort, you can make what interests you interesting for your audience.

When you have difficulty finding a subject that interests you, try a technique called *brainstorming*. Take out a blank sheet of paper and jot down as many potential speech topics as you can. Try to keep your pen nearly constantly writing and don't judge your ideas or the quality of these topics; aim for quantity. After you have listed as many as you can, put the sheet away for at least 8 hr. When you return to it, you may very well find that you have listed a number of topics of interest to you that you hadn't thought about.

Am I Qualified to Speak on This Subject?

What are your qualifications for dealing with a particular subject? The fact that you are interested in a subject does not necessarily mean that you are qualified to speak on it. If your interest is recent, you might lack sufficient knowledge or experience to prepare the subject effectively. In some cases, it might be better to select a subject with which you are more familiar. Are you qualified because of background or skill? Do you speak from personal experience? What are your credentials? Do you have special skills in real estate, music, computers, or sewing? Sometimes, the perfect speech topic is so close that the speaker doesn't see it. A speech by a student in the dental technology program on caring for your teeth will undoubtedly be well received by the student's classmates. If you have expertise or special knowledge or experience about your speech topic, indicate this to your audience in your introduction. If you have access to special information through a friend or relative who is an expert, indicate this as well. Even if your knowledge about the topic comes only through research, you want to let your audience know that what you are telling them is accurate and carefully prepared.

Will My Audience Find This Subject Interesting?

It takes little effort to pay attention to a subject that is interesting. Therefore, you will hold the attention of your audience if your subject is interesting to them. If you are not sure it will be, you must work to make it so. Reflect on what you know about your audience and try to have some connection between your topic and their interests.

Will My Audience Find This Subject Useful?

People will willingly pay attention to a communication if they expect to gain something useful from doing so. Consider your own experience. Have you ever followed a set of instructions on how to use a computer program, assemble a bicycle, or play a board game? Have you ever attended a lecture on what to expect on the final exam? Have you ever bought a do-it-yourself book and tried to follow the *simplified instructions*? Did you pay attention? Of course you did. If the subject you choose will benefit your audience in some way, it will quite likely hold their attention. If you feel that the usefulness of your subject will not be readily apparent to your audience, tell them in your introduction how they will benefit from listening to your speech. The result of doing this simple task is a much more focused and attentive audience.

Is My Subject Sufficiently Narrowed?

In most cases, you will be given a definite time limit when you are asked to give a speech. If you exceed this time limit significantly, you are bound to annoy your audience. Many beginning speakers try to cover too much in the time available to them. It is far better to deal with a restricted subject in detail than to cover too many points. Remember, if you cover too much material without supporting it adequately, your audience is unlikely to remember it, no matter how long your speech is.

SPECIFIC PURPOSE

After you have chosen your subject in accordance with the considerations above, you are ready to formulate a specific purpose. Earlier the general purposes for speaking, namely to entertain, to inform, and to persuade, were listed. Specific purposes tell more precisely what your intent is. They indicate in more detail exactly what you hope to accomplish. Note the following examples:

1. *General Purpose:* to entertain
   Specific purposes
   a. to amuse my audience by explaining how to wash a bull elephant
   b. to hold my audience in suspense while telling of the time I was robbed
   c. to amaze my audience with a demonstration of magic
   d. to fascinate my audience with a story about my first parachute jump.
2. *General Purpose:* to inform
   Specific purposes
   a. to explain the art of tree dwarfing
   b. to demonstrate how to make an omelet
   c. to show how to take an effective snapshot
   d. to report the results of a recent experiment.
3. *General Purpose:* to persuade
   Specific purposes
   a. to motivate my audience to contribute to Mothers Against Drunk Driving
   b. to prove to my audience that my new plan for ending the arms race will work
   c. to increase my audience's reverence for our flag
   d. to modify my audience's attitude about socialized medicine.

Note that the specific purposes are phrases that begin with the infinitive form of a verb, which clearly relates to one of the three general purposes of speech. Thus, speeches to entertain, amuse, fascinate, amaze, delight; speeches to inform explain, make clear, demonstrate, report; and speeches to persuade motivate, prove, increase, modify.

THE CENTRAL IDEA

Once you have phrased your specific purpose statement, it is time to develop your central idea. The central idea may be thought of as the thesis, the key statement, or what you would like your audience to remember from your speech. Although it is related to the speech purpose, it is worded differently. A specific purpose statement is worded as a phrase. A central idea is a one-sentence statement around which the entire speech is developed. The following guidelines will help you in developing your central idea statement.

The Central Idea Should Be a Complete Sentence

In most cases, a central idea should be stated as a simple complete sentence. Phrases, questions, or compound and complex sentences are usually not appropriate for central ideas.

> *Good:*   Being a single parent is tough.
>
> (Simple, declarative sentence)
>
> *Bad:*   Are single parents getting a bad rap?
>
> (Question)
>
> *Bad:*   Single parent problems
>
> (Phrase)
>
> *Bad:*   After I raised Alex, I discovered being a single parent is tough.
>
> (Complex sentence)

The Central Idea Should Be a Statement You Must Explain or Defend

Your central idea should be a statement that requires clarification or reinforcement. Once you have developed your central idea, your next step will be to choose main points to support it. Following that, you will choose supporting points to support the main points, and so on. Therefore, you must develop your central idea with thoughtfulness and care so that the supports that you use will seem clear and logical to your audience.

In some cases, your central idea will break up quite naturally into three or four main points or logical divisions. For example, consider a speech with the central idea "Walking is the ideal exercise." You might support it with these three main points: (1) it can be done by almost anyone at any age, (2) it conditions the mind and body, and (3) it removes unwanted fat. In other cases, the main points supporting your central idea might be a series of steps like the four steps involved in making lasagna, the three steps in refinishing furniture, and so on. Perhaps the main points supporting your central idea will be the reasons you give to convince your audience that your central idea is true.

The Central Idea Should Be Specific

State the central idea in specific rather than general terms. When you give your audience terms that are instantly understandable to them at the outset of your speech, they will be able to follow you more easily, and you won't have to waste their time defining terms for them as you unfold your ideas.

> *Vague:*   The U.S. Social Security System is in crisis.
>
> *Specific:*   The five-step Ball Plan can save Social Security.

The Central Idea Should Cover a Single Topic

Combining more than one topic in a speech will create frustration and confusion for both the speaker and the audience.

Bad: Unless we stop the influx of drugs into this country and stiffen the penalties for using and dealing, drug use by our youth will double in the next 5 years.

Good: There are three steps that must be taken to stop the influx of drugs into this country.

The Central Idea Should Be Audience-Centered

Since you developed your subject and purpose with your audience in mind, you must show them that you considered them carefully when phrasing your central idea statement.

Good: Walking is the ideal exercise.

   (Includes practically everyone)

Bad: Walking is a good way to shed those extra pounds.

   (Not everyone is overweight and someone who is might resent the comment.)

The Central Idea Should Relate to Purpose

Stating the central idea as a complete sentence will help you plan your communication more effectively. Following are three central idea statements related to three of the specific purpose statements:

1. *Specific Purpose:* to amuse my audience by telling them how to wash a bull elephant.
   a. *Central Idea*—Washing a bull elephant isn't all that easy.
2. *Specific purpose:* to explain the art of tree dwarfing.
   a. *Central Idea*—The secret of tree dwarfing is twofold: cutting the root and branch system properly and maintaining the tree correctly.
3. *Specific Purpose:* to motivate my audience to contribute to CARE.
   a. *Central Idea*—CARE is the most efficient and effective charity in the world.

As you can see, the central idea statement is a clear statement of the way in which you plan to develop your speech. For example, the first purpose above is to entertain, specifically to amuse, the audience by telling them how to wash a bull elephant. The central idea—Washing a bull elephant isn't all that easy—implies that the speech will involve some of the humorous problems that could arise when trying to wash the elephant. The second purpose—to explain the art of tree dwarfing—is to inform. Its central idea indicates that the speech will deal with the two most important principles in tree dwarfing: cutting the roots and branches properly and maintaining the tree correctly. The third specific purpose—to motivate my audience to contribute to CARE—is to activate. The central idea clearly indicates that you will develop the speech by talking about the efficiency and effectiveness of CARE.

DISCUSSION QUESTIONS

1. Tell of a time when an internal distraction kept you from concentrating on a speech or lecture. Did you try to overcome the barrier? What did you do?
2. Tell of an instance when an external distraction kept you from concentrating on a speech or lecture. Was the problem eventually solved?
3. Have you ever been in a situation when your bias toward the speaker kept you from maintaining attention to the speech? Did you overcome the problem?

EXERCISES

1. State whether the primary purpose in each of the following situations is (a) to inform, (b) to entertain, (c) to convince, (d) to reinforce, or (e) to activate. Be prepared to explain and defend your answer.
   a. A newscast
   b. A beer commercial
   c. A debate
   d. A eulogy
   e. A soap opera
   f. A circus parade
2. Below are three specific purposes. Which is best and why?
   a. To tell about the tennis tournament, The Australian Open.
   b. To have my audience to understand the importance of buying local.
   c. To persuade my audience that the Chevy Volt is the best car produced.
3. Select an online speech video to view and translate the speaker's main ideas and important supporting details into your own words and write out a full sentence outline detailing the speech. Later, discuss the purpose, subject, central idea, and major purpose of the speech.

4 The Introduction and Conclusion

OBJECTIVES OF INTRODUCTIONS

Now that you have determined your purpose and subject, you are ready to begin developing your introduction. In most cases, an introduction to a speech has five objectives: (1) it should capture the audience's attention, (2) it should present the central idea of the speech, (3) it should indicate your qualifications, (4) it should give the audience a reason for listening, and (5) it should preview the ideas to be covered in the speech. Keep in mind that although an introduction will often include all five of these elements, at times one or more of them may be omitted.

1. *Capture Attention* The first goal of the speaker is to get the attention of the audience. You cannot communicate to an audience that is not paying attention to you. Ten suggestions for getting the attention of your audience are given in the next section. They are designed to put your audience in a good frame of mind and to prepare them to listen to you.

2. *Present Central Idea* You should present the central idea of your speech early in your introduction. It should be a declarative statement about your subject that you must explain or defend rather than a fact that no one can deny. The central idea may be thought of as the key statement or idea of your speech. It should be worded as a simple sentence.

3. *Indicate Your Qualifications* If you can show your audience that you have appreciable knowledge about your subject, it will motivate them to listen to you. If you've always had an interest in the subject and researched it carefully, reveal this to your

audience. If you have had personal experience with a topic, tell them about it. If you are an expert on a subject, don't be modest about it, let them know.

4. *Give Reason for Listening* The next step is to make it clear to the audience why they should listen to your speech. You might show how a problem affects them or others they are concerned about and why they need to listen to your plan for solving the problem; you might explain why the subject is useful to them and how they will gain something by listening; or you might give them some background information that will trigger their curiosity or interest.

5. *Preview Main Points* The preview statement gives your audience a clear explanation of the main ideas to be covered in your speech. It is important because it prepares your audience to listen for and retain key information. The preview statement is the last thing you say in the introduction and should provide a transition into the body of the speech. If you've prepared your speech carefully with your audience in mind, your preview statement will hold the attention of your audience and give them something to look forward to.

ATTENTION STEP IN INTRODUCTIONS

Besides fulfilling some or all of these objectives, an effective introduction should lead smoothly into the body of the speech. The first objective of the introduction is to get the attention of the audience. Following are 10 methods for accomplishing this. Each is followed by a model.

Start Off with Humor

When I was preparing this speech, I was reminded of the story of the man who goes to a confessional booth to tell the priest about an indiscretion.

> A man goes into a confessional booth and tells the priest, "Father, I'm sixty-five years old and up to now I've always been faithful to my wife. But last weekend I went to my alma mater's football game. I met a young coed at the game and we wound up at a motel, where we made love not only once but two times." "Well, that's pretty heavy my son. You better see your own priest for penance on that one." "I don't have a priest," the guy replies. "I'm Jewish." "You're Jewish," the priest says. "Then what are you telling me for?" "I'm telling everyone!" the man responds.

Well, to many that story might be funny, but to others it hits all too close to home. And that fact is brought out by the alarmingly high divorce rate in this country. This morning I am going to give you some useful tips on how to have and hold a successful marriage.

Begin with a Brief Story

I was playing cards with a group of friends the other night and Bob, one of the card players, said, "Peter, have I ever shown you a picture of my grandchildren?" And, Peter, replied, "No and I'd like to thank you." I could tell from the expression on his face that Bob was miffed by the comment. And I thought to myself, "You know, we're getting insensitive to the feeling of others."

What Peter should have said was, "No, but I'd love to see them," and looked at the pictures making a few complimentary remarks about each of the grandchildren; perhaps that would have made Bob happy, avoiding an uncomfortable situation for all. We kept playing cards for awhile, but that exchange cast a pall on the card game and it ended soon afterward, much earlier than usual.

This situation could have been easily avoided. Man is basically a self-centered creature. No one interests us so much as ourselves. In order to get along with others, you must show them that you respect the things they're interested in. Today I'm going to show you what you can do to get along well with others.

Ask a Rhetorical Question

Do we really believe that all men are created equal?

Certainly, not all of us do. One of the major problems in this country and around the world is the problem of racism. Whether overt or hidden, it is destructive. Countless wars have been fought because of racism, and although governments and religious organizations have tried to deal with it, little success has been achieved. Today, I am going to have you take a short test to let you see whether you have any racist tendencies. The test will be private and you will be the only one who knows the answer.

Begin with a Statistic

Untreated mental illnesses cost this country more than $80 billion annually in lost productivity unemployment, broken lives and broken families, needless hospitalization, unnecessary use of jails and imprisonment, and homelessness. It is the number one reason for hospitalization nationwide. However, in the last 10 years, there have been major breakthroughs in understanding the nature of mental illness. Today I'm going to tell you what these breakthroughs are.

Refer to a Previous Speaker

I really enjoyed Carl's speech about getting drunk drivers off the road. The problem in this country is horrendous, but it is solvable. Tougher laws have worked in other countries. As Carl pointed out, the auto industry is so powerful that it has influenced our legislators to resist the public's demand for tougher laws. Today I'm going to tell you what you can do to help stop this madness.

Refer to Familiar Terms

Of all the dangers to our environment, air pollution is the most alarming. We can live for a week without food and 3 days without water but only 4 min without air. Today I'm going to tell you how air pollution has contributed to global warming, and what you can do to address the problem.

Begin with a Definition

Mental illness refers to a group of brain disorders that cause disturbances in thinking, feeling, and relating, often causing an inability to cope with the ordinary demands of life. The major mental illnesses are schizophrenia, bipolar disorder, major depression, schizoaffective disorder, anxiety disorder, obsessive compulsive disorder, and borderline personality disorder. Twenty-five percent of American families are affected by mental illness. Today I'm going to tell you what you can do if you are affected by it.

Begin with a Startling Statement

The greatest threat to our future is the destruction of our environment. Unless we reduce the emissions of greenhouse gases into the atmosphere, we will destroy the earth's ozone layer and end all life on our planet. Time is running out. We must do something soon before it's too late. Today I'm going to tell you what you can do to deal with this terrible problem.

Start with a Quotation

It was Winston Churchill, prime minister of England during World War II, who said, "Kites rise higher against the wind, not with it." Since the terrorist attack on the World Trade Center on September 11, 2001, the attitude of too many has been to retaliate against those responsible. This resulted in our getting mired in Afghanistan and invading Iraq. It also has resulted in our increasing our military budget 12%, to $481.4 billion plus $141.7 billion to continue to fight the war on terror. Thus, the United States spends considerably more than our allies, and Russia, China, North Korea, Iran, and Afghanistan combined. For years we were in an arms race with the Soviet Union. Now we seem to be in an arms race with ourselves.

List a Series of Examples

On their way home from a family reunion, a young couple and their infant son are killed in a head-on collision with a pickup truck that crosses the center line. Two weeks later, an 8-year-old girl is crippled for life by a car that jumps the curb, crashes through a fence, and veers into the yard where she is playing. The next day, after leaving a party, a teenage girl and her drunken boyfriend are thrown from his motorcycle and killed when he fails to negotiate a dangerous curve. What do these accidents have in common? They were all caused by drivers who were intoxicated. They are typical stories that appear in newspapers day after day in cities throughout our nation. And the greatest tragedy is that many of these kinds of accidents would never happen again if we could do one thing: find a way to get the drunk driver off the road.

The list of suggestions given above for attention-getting introductions is by no means complete. Other methods include referring to a recent event or one that is soon to take place, a buildup of suspense, the use of a visual aid as part of the introduction, the use of novelty or the unusual, an introduction involving conflict, and establishing a common ground with the audience.

Choose your introduction carefully. It should be consistent with the purpose and the central idea of your speech. A humorous introduction to a serious speech would be a poor choice. Be aware that the introduction is the first thing your audience hears, and therefore it has much to do with the effectiveness of your speech.

TYPES OF CONCLUSIONS

Some people feel that the conclusion is the most important part of the speech. It is your last chance to achieve your purpose, and it signals to your audience that your speech is ending. Plan your conclusion carefully. It is the final impression the audience will get of your speech, and it should leave them with a sense of completeness. It is no accident that many of the most memorable lines from speeches have occurred at or near the conclusion. Among them are the following:

> I know not what course others may take, but as for me, give me liberty, or give me death!
>
> —Patrick Henry

> That we here highly resolve that these dead shall not have died in vain—that this nation, under God, shall have a new birth of freedom—and that the government of the people, by the people, and for the people shall not perish from the earth.
>
> —Abraham Lincoln

> Ask not what your country can do for you; ask what you can do for your country.
>
> —John F. Kennedy

Finally, remember never to introduce new material in your conclusion. To do so will leave your audience with the impression that you failed to plan your speech carefully and added the new material as an afterthought, or that you left something out of your talk and remembered it just as you were about to close. Either way, you wind up diminishing your presentational impact. Following are six suggestions for effectively concluding your speech.

End with a Call to Action

There must be an all-out effort to deal with mental illness in this country. Jails and prisons have become the greatest providers of mental health services. Each community is going to have to commit the money it will take to accomplish this huge undertaking, and we must prod the federal government into doing more, and also do more to seek private donations for this worthwhile effort. Here are some specific things that we as private citizens must do.

End with a Rhetorical Question

A speech with the central idea "We need the help of every citizen to combat global warming: Can the United States continue to watch the atmospheric CO_2 levels rise dangerously higher without doing more to address it? Obviously, the answer is no. There are a variety of things that must be done to combat this problem and each of us has a job to do. Here are 10 specific things that each of you can do."

End with a Positive Vision of the Future

The vision of the future that you project can be either positive or negative. The choice is up to you. For instance, in a problem–solution speech, you can visualize for your audience what the future will be like once the problem is solved.

The cure for mental illness is out there. Someone has to find it and someone will. Organizations like the National Alliance for the Mentally Ill (NAMI) and the National Association for Research on Schizophrenia and Depression (NARSAD) offer significant hope to people who suffer from this terrible disease. Remember, mental illness affects one out of every four families nationwide, but there is hope.

End with a Restatement of Your Central Idea

A speech that has as its central idea that we can't continue to deal with the threat to terrorism we face by increasing our military budget each year, might end this way:

The 2008 military budget of $481.4 billion increased the 2007 budget by 12% and the 2009 budget request of $515.4 billion was a $35.9 billion increase over that. When are we going to wake up to the fact that the only way we are going to make the world safer is to aid those in the world who are in need?

End with a Summary of the Main Ideas Developed in Your Speech

A speech with the central idea that mental illness can be devastating, but that for many, recovery is possible, might conclude this way:

As I stand here speaking to you today there are researchers working on new medications and treatments in universities and medical research institutions throughout the world. New psychotropic drugs are being tested right now. The cure for mental illness is out there. Someone has to find it and someone will. You can count on it. Remember, first, mental illness can happen to anyone at any age—no one is immune. Second, most people have little knowledge or understanding of mental illness. Third, there is a great deal of stigma attached to this biological brain disorder. Fourth, there are organizations that help those who are affected deal with mental illness. And, fifth, new discoveries in research and treatment offer greater hope for recovery. We start the 21st century with better treatment for mental illness and more help available. Remember, mental illness affects one out of four families, but there is hope. Mental illness can be devastating, but for many, recovery is possible.

End with a Negative Vision of the Future

There may be times when you will want to leave your audience with the feeling that the problem must be solved before it is too late. In these cases, you might want to paint a picture of what the future will be like if something is not done to solve the problem as soon as possible. The speech that has as its central idea that racism is evil might end this way:

> We are living in two societies: one White, the other, Black and Hispanic, separate and unequal. Black and Latino babies in the United States are 300% more likely to grow up in poverty than white babies. America has a D-grade on race and equality. It is time we do something about this. Each of us has a responsibility to work for the common good. This morning I am going to tell you what each of us can do to address this important problem.

Other suggestions for concluding your speech are to end with a quotation, poem, story, or startling statement.

SAMPLE FULL-SENTENCE OUTLINE FOR A SPEECH TO INSTRUCT

The following is a sample full-sentence outline of a speech to instruct on the contributions African Americans have made to their country.

Black is Beautiful

Introduction
 I. Did you know that there were more than 5,000 African American cowboys in the Old West, and that an African American named Bill Pickett invented the technique of "bulldogging"? Are you aware that African American participation in the development of this country began in the early 1600s? (Attention getters)

II I learned quite a few interesting facts such as these when I attended a series of lectures on campus during Black History week last semester. Since then, I've been reading a lot and browsing the Internet learning about African American heroes. (Indicate qualifications)

III. I learned that African Americans have contributed significantly to this nation's development. (Central idea statement) I was amazed, though somewhat disappointed, that I hadn't heard these things before.

IV. The record shows that African American men and women have been in the forefront of our progress as a nation throughout the years. These are things everyone should know about the U.S. history. (Reason for listening)

V. That's why I'm going to tell you about some famous African Americans and also about some lesser known African Americans who have contributed to our growth, have dedicated themselves to our welfare, and have added to the quality of life here in this land of ours. (Preview statement)

Body

I. Throughout our history, African American men and women have contributed significantly to the growth of the United States.
   A. African Americans were instrumental in developing this country.
      1. African Americans sailed with Columbus on his voyages to the New World.
      2. African Americans were with Coronado in New Mexico and De Soto in Alabama.
      3. York, an African American slave, traveled with Lewis and Clark on their Northwest Passage to the Pacific.
      4. Jean Baptiste DuSable, an African American, founded Chicago.
   B. African Americans have furthered industrial expansion in the United States. Four significant contributions were as follows:
      1. Lewis Latimer invented the first long-lasting light bulb and the safety elevator.
      2. Granville T. Woods invented the third rail.
      3. Garrett Augustus Morgan invented the gas mask.
      4. Shelby J. Davidson invented the adding machine.
II. Over the years, African Americans have been dedicated to the welfare of the United States.
   A. African Americans have served illustriously in defending our country.
      1. Over 5,000 African Americans served in the Continental Army.
      2. African Americans fought with valor in the War of 1812.
      3. In World War I, 370,000 African Americans served their country with valor.
         a. The 369th received more citations than any other regiment.
         b. The 369th, 370th, and 371st were awarded France's highest honor.

    4. Over one million African Americans enlisted in World War II.
      a. The all-African American Panther tank battalion overwhelmed the Nazis.
      b. Benjamin O. Davis became the nation's first African American general.

B. African American religious and political leaders have enriched our values.
    1. Frederick Douglass worked with and influenced eight presidents.
    2. Reverend Martin Luther King, Jr., stirred the soul of the United States with his dream of equality for all.
    3. Shirley Chisholm became the first African American woman to be elected to Congress, fought tirelessly for the rights of the disenfranchised.
    4. Reverend Jesse Jackson has been an outspoken advocate of social, political, and economic justice for all.

C. African Americans have contributed significantly in the field of medicine.
    1. Dr. Daniel Hale Williams performed America's first open-heart operation.
    2. George Washington Carver found over 400 uses for the peanut and sweet potato.
    3. Dr. Benjamin Carson was the first neurosurgeon to separate Siamese twins joined at the head.
    4. Dr. Charles Drew, an expert on blood plasma, set up the first blood bank.

III. From the outset, African Americans have contributed to the quality of life in our country.

A. African American contributions to the cultural arts have been impressive.
    1. Marion Anderson, the first African American to sing at the Metropolitan Opera, won the National Medal of Arts.
    2. Alex Haley was awarded the Pulitzer Prize in 1977 for his novel, *Roots*.
    3. Sydney Poitier won the 1963 Best Actor Academy Award for his performance in *Lilies of the Field*.
    4. Maya Angelou, author of *I Know Why the Caged Bird Sings*, was awarded the National Book Award.

B. African Americans have excelled in the area of sports.
    1. Jack Johnson won the world heavyweight boxing championship in 1903.
    2. Jesse Owens was the first athlete to win four gold medals in the Olympics.
    3. Hank Aaron set a world record with 755 home runs.
    4. Jackie Joyner-Kersee was declared world's greatest female athlete after winning six medals at the 1988 summer Olympics.

   C. African American entertainers have shown remarkable talent.
1. Harry Belafonte—world renowned singer—has won two Emmy Awards.
2. Cicely Tyson won an Emmy for Best Actress of the Year in 1974 for her role in *The Autobiography of Miss Jane Pittman*.
3. Bill Cosby was named the *entertainer of the twentieth century*.
4. Denzel Washington, a matinee idol of the 1990s, won an Academy Award in 1989 for his performance in the Civil War film *Glory*.

Conclusion

   I. This nation owes a debt of gratitude to African Americans who have helped to develop and defend this country, have been dedicated to its welfare, and have added to the quality of life of its citizens. (Summary of main points)
   II. African Americans have made significant inroads in the field of medicine, impressive contributions in fine arts, sports, and entertainment and have enriched our values.
   III. Many African American actors, musicians, and writers are world renowned. It is easy to see why the words *Black* and *beautiful* are synonymous.
   IV. I hope I have introduced you to some African American heroes you hadn't heard of and that you now have a better understanding of how different people in this country have worked together for the common good.

Bibliography

Abdul-Jabbar, Kareem. *Black Profiles in Courage*. New York: William Morrow, 1996.

Brodie, James. *Created Equal: The Lives and Ideas of Black American Innovators*. New York: William Morrow, 1993.

Haber, Louis. *Black Pioneers of Science and Invention*. New York: Harcourt Brace and World, 1970.

Harrison, Paul C. *Black Light: The African-American Hero*. New York: Thunder's Mouth Press, 1993.

Lee, George L. *Interesting People: Black American History Makers*. New York: Ballantine Books, 1989.

Potter, Joan. *African-American Firsts*. Elizabethtown, NY: Pinto Press, 1994.

Stewart, Jeffery C. *1001 Things Everyone Should Know About African-American History*. New York: Doubleday, 1996.

Although an outline for your speech similar to the one above involves a great deal of preparation, it is important for a number of reasons. First, it provides a logical arrangement of your main points and subpoints along with an idea of the supporting materials you are going to use. This will enable you to determine whether your ideas flow smoothly from one to another, and whether you have included a well-balanced and sufficient number of the six kinds of supporting materials. Second, it will provide a framework from which you can prepare note cards or a phrase outline, or from which you can write out a speech to be delivered from manuscript or from memory.

This outline includes a bibliography. While many of the speeches you deliver will involve your own experience, there are times when you will want to include materials you have gathered through research. In these cases, or whenever your instructor so directs, attach a bibliography to your preparation outline.

INTRODUCTION AND CONCLUSION FINAL THOUGHT

When assessing your introduction, and conclusion and its relation to your speech, remember the well-proven formula for delivering effective information which I refer to as the "one, two, three sucker punch." (1) Tell the audience what you are going to talk about (introduction, preview main points), (2) tell them (body of the speech), and (3) tell them what you told them (conclusion, summary of main ideas). This simple formula increases your audience's retention of your information—and since we know the importance of being audience centered, the result is powerful.

DISCUSSION QUESTIONS

1. Discuss some methods of getting your audience's attention in the introduction.
2. Discuss the different types of conclusions detailed. Do you think one style is superior?
3. Why do you think introductions and conclusions are so important for successful speeches?

EXERCISES

1. With the help of group of your peers, write an introduction for the speech: "Why Coca-Cola is the most successful soft drink manufacturer."
2. With the help of a group of your peers, write a conclusion for "The reasons college students should use hybrid cars."
3. In a small group, describe a speech you have recently heard. What did the speaker do to capture your attention? Did it work?

5 Gathering Supportive Material

Chapter 3 suggested that you choose a subject that suits the purpose of your speech and that is interesting to you. Picking topics that are of personal interest often correlates with more passion in your speaking voice and in turn a more engaged and receptive audience. Spending time honing in a speaking topic that is important to you is vital because you will spend a significant amount of effort collecting facts and gathering ideas for your speech, followed by organizing the information and constructing your speech. Try to examine a wide variety of resources to help represent your topic.

You can collect information for your speech in a number of ways: (1) develop it from your own knowledge and experience, (2) access it from written sources primarily through a library, (3) gather it through electronic resources, and (4) acquire it through interviews.

PERSONAL EXPERIENCE AND KNOWLEDGE

If the subject you have chosen is from your own experience or knowledge, then this is the first place to start when gathering supporting material for your speech. Keep in mind that your experiences include not only your personal involvement with, or observation of, events as they occurred, but also those things you have experienced vicariously by reading or hearing about them. There are a number of ways to use personal experience when planning your speech. First, you can develop a speech to entertain in which you tell a story about something exciting, suspenseful, fascinating, unusual, or humorous that has happened to you.

Second, you can develop a persuasive speech to make a point in which you tell your audience about an experience you had that taught you a lesson. In the speech of personal experience, there are two possible approaches to make a point: (1) the main idea (the point) is stated at the beginning of the speech followed by a story that reinforces it, and (2) the story is told first, and the point is made at the conclusion of the speech. Thus, you might say, "I learned at an early age never to trust strangers," and tell your audience about an experience you had that taught you this lesson, or you might relate the experience first and end by saying, "and that's how I learned never to trust strangers."

Finally, you can use your own experience and knowledge to compile a list of ideas on a particular topic. If your own knowledge or experience qualifies you as somewhat of an expert in a particular area, you might be the only resource needed to develop your speech. Even if you are not an expert, you may be amazed at the amount of information you can come up with when brainstorming a topic with which you are familiar. If your list of ideas comes entirely from your own knowledge or experience, you might be able to develop your speech without doing any further research. In most cases, however, you will have to do some research to add to the materials you already have. Keep in mind that you may choose to do your speech on a topic you find interesting but know little about. In this case, before brainstorming, you will want to do preliminary research not only to gather ideas but also to determine whether there is sufficient material available to develop an effective speech on that topic.

BRAINSTORMING

Brainstorming is an excellent technique for generating ideas on your subject. The principle is to come up with as many ideas as possible about your topic as fast as you can think of them. Write them all down. Pay no attention to their quality and don't evaluate them. Don't worry if some seem irrelevant; you can discard them later. After you have listed as many ideas as you can, you are ready for step two: clustering.

CLUSTERING

In step two, you put your topic down and write down all the ideas you have come up with on your brainstorming list that relate to it. Analyze the list carefully. See if you can identify any ideas as main points, supporting points, or subpoints for your speech. Use arrows to indicate their relationships to each other as shown in Figure 5.1.

The cluster of words around the topic "walking" reflects your concept of the benefits of walking. You see walking as being healthy, inexpensive, convenient, and so on. Keep in mind that as you develop the cluster into a framework for your speech, not everything will be used. Some things will be left out and others will be changed. The important thing is that you have begun to

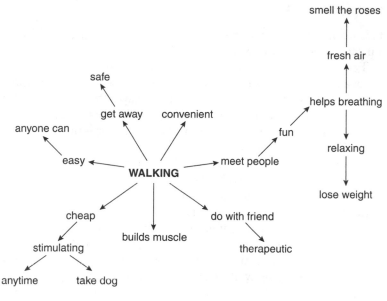

FIGURE 5.1 Clustering

gather ideas for your speech. Now you can consider ways to locate material other than through your own knowledge and experience. Consider interviewing someone you know who walks daily. How about your Uncle Jeff? Your cousin Stacie? That old guy you see walking his dog around campus every morning? Those stories conveyed in your final speech make for compelling segments sure to grab the interest of your audience.

THE LIBRARY

It is a mistake to think that because of the computer you no longer need to access the library. The Internet has significantly changed the way libraries operate and you may not have to physically enter the brick and mortar library building to take advantage of many of your library resources. It is important to note that your library has databases and information that is not attainable from standard Internet searches. Even in an era of digital dominance, the tangible resources and books in the library are also great resources for your speech.

Many colleges spend millions of dollars annually to have access to the most current of professional databases. Most college students do not realize that a portion of their student fees are often utilized to subscribe to these databases. The research that can be gained from college research databases is often coveted information that many private businesses pay hefty sums to obtain. Unfortunately, your access to these databases is not indefinite. Most access to college databases ends after your college enrollment: make the most out of your database access. It is beyond valuable.

RESEARCH DATABASES

Research databases are fairly user friendly to navigate. From your library home page you can access the databases. Often the databases are listed alphabetically as well as categorized by field. If you are interested in understanding about Starbucks free trade coffee, you may want to search the business databases, typing in keywords you find relevant: perhaps "free trade." After searching the databases, you will find many of the articles that are in full text (often .pdf) and they are downloadable, printable, and can be e-mailed. Often databases go back 10 or more years.

Effectively using your library resources doesn't stop at research databases. Connecting to your library's web-based catalog to locate books, periodicals, and customized reading lists is also an important tool. But perhaps the most important resource in any library is the librarian. Librarians know how to help you find the information you need. Most libraries have at least one reference librarian. Reference librarians are experts in locating obscure information that evades common Internet searches. They are almost always experts in searching databases as well. If you can't locate that elusive fact or detail from your search efforts, it is well worth your time to talk to a reference librarian. Many libraries have the option of live chat services that enable you to ask for information from a reference librarian in a convenient-to-use manner over your computer or phone. These services will save you a trip to the library when you're looking for the author of an obscure poem, the date of a particular event, a question involving usage or grammar, and so on. Most libraries also have brochures listing the research services they provide. Do yourself and your research a favor and take the time to seek out the various options available to you.

ADVANCED ONLINE SEARCHING

Getting the best information from your Internet search engine is an art form. A disadvantage of the vastness of the Internet is that many people find the sheer amount of information overwhelming. For good reason—it is. Plugging in a couple words into Google often gets a string of nearly unlimited information. But it is the savvy Internet searcher, who really knows how to use the tools, who can find the gems. It is finding the correct and appropriate information that will allow your presentation to stand out and engage the audience.

If you are clumsy with your searching, and think just typing in: *college tuition* is the best way to obtain information on college tuition as it relates to you, you have some learning to do. Boolean searches, named after the 1800s British-born Irish mathematician George Boole, created a way to get to more appropriate data. By looking at the relationship between search terms, the Boolean method figures out where to pinpoint the appropriateness of Internet search results.

Experienced Internet researchers know the Boolean method, and the vernacular—since it pays off in dividends. Originally Boolean was defined as using OR, AND, and NOT to help eliminate subjects that were not relevant.

But just like nearly everything Internet-related, Boolean has evolved along with the digital revolution. Google did away with NOT and replaced the parameter with "–". The negative sign is to directly precede the word you want your search to exclude such as (–this). Currently most Internet searches, such as Google, still respond to OR, AND, and "–".

Let's dig deeper with the college tuition analogy. You need to find several resources pertaining to college tuition for a presentation.

- college OR tuition
  - This search finds articles that discuss either college or tuition. OR expands the amount of information a search returns.
- college AND tuition
  - This search finds articles that address college and tuition. AND limits the search and decreases the results.
- college –tuition
  - This search finds articles that are exclusively about college. –tuition tells the browser to not bring up anything with the word tuition.

Another valuable tool for search engine success is the double quotation mark.

Double Quotation Marks: When using double quotations around "a phrase" or "word," it implies exact match to the search engines.

wind power USA = brings in 30,200,000 hits and overwhelm the search engine as it is looking for any combination of the words.

"wind power USA" = brings the tally to under 1,000,000 specifically looking at sites that have the exact phrase.

"wind power USA" AND "Great Lakes" = chisels the return to 17,000.

"wind power USA" AND "Great Lakes" – turbine = brings the return to 6,000.

As you begin to locate strong information for your support material, it is vital that you bookmark the URL address on your browser so that you can get back to the information. If you cut and paste material out of a site, which is not recommended, it is imperative that you label that information with a citation instantly. After cutting and pasting information, many people lose track of what information they "found" and what information they actually created themselves. You need to be cognizant of where information originated. Many people, in cutting and pasting, utilize different colors for the text so that it is a visual reminder that the information (a) isn't your own and (b) needs to be cited appropriately.

PRESENTATIONS FOR THE 2.0

You have searched out the best possible sources for your subject. You knew how to get to the exact information you were seeking thanks to Boolean searching. You found relevant databases that had great resources, and your librarian helped you find some great leads on a nice online graph. In other words, you have the support material—but how will you use it in the classroom?

If your classroom has a computer and data projector, you may want to bring some of your visuals as digital files. USB thumb drives are great for holding pictures, images, and even small video segments. As a presenter, like a parachuter, it is a good plan to always have more than one method—just in case. If you are using USB, try to also send files to your e-mail so they can be pulled up if needed. As a general rule, you should be able to have your files, videos, and charts pulled up and ready to use in under 25 seconds. Like every other aspect of your speech, you need to practice this at home, or on other campus computers, to make sure this process is streamlined and efficient. Directly before a speech is no time to question the location of a file or how it will come up on the computer.

Should you have an Apple computer, it is your responsibility to have the video converter purchased and with you to allow your computer to interact with the classroom video system. Classroom systems are nearly always PC-based and do not adapt to Apple computers without a special adapter.

YOUTUBE

If you find a short segment of a YouTube video, and the classroom capability is there, you may want to talk to your instructor as to if this is an appropriate form of visual aid. Many people have found that short videos around 30 seconds or less have a great impact. If you have been given the go-ahead and are allowed to utilize this method, you should consider creating a Youtube.com account.

By creating an account with YouTube, you allow yourself the ability to create playlists in specific folders that hold your video selections. It might be useful to create a playlist for your speech. By doing this, all you need to do on your speech day is sign-in to Youtube.com and pull up the specific folder. This playlist alleviates the process of searching for a video in front of a classroom full of onlookers.

ETHICS IN USING THE INTERNET

Do not assume that the information you are accessing from the Internet is always credible. Because information on the Internet can be biased or inaccurate, it is your ethical responsibility to check the material you will be using in your speeches carefully. If it comes from a source that is unbiased and reputable, then most likely the material you are accessing is valid. However, anyone can launch a website on the Internet. There are many thousands of new sites started each day. Since the Internet is not owned or regulated by anyone, there are no organizational rules to ensure accuracy or relevance. Unfortunately, in some cases, websites are filled with fallacious or useless content. Furthermore, there is the issue of stability. A website that was there one day may be gone or in a different location the next. This means you must be careful to investigate the credibility and relevance of the material you have found.

Use common sense when evaluating the site you are accessing. Ask yourself these questions:

1. Is the information accurate? Who provided it? Is it documented or verifiable?
2. Is the information objective? Does the organization sponsoring the site have any interests or bias that would cause them to put misleading information on its website?
3. Is the information reliable? What are the author's qualifications? If no author is listed, is the website established by a reliable source such as a reputable organization, government agency, or university?
4. Is the information current? When was it published? Is there a more recent version? If no date is given, the information may be outdated.

If there is any question in your mind as to whether the information you will be using in your speech is accurate, objective, reliable, or up-to-date, don't use it. Above all, be suspicious of sites that have grammatical or typographical errors. If you have any misgivings and cannot verify your information, don't use it.

INTERVIEWING

An interview can be an effective and interesting way to gather information. Up-to-date information from an expert in the field can often carry a great deal of weight and engage the audience. Faculty members, clergy, community leaders, and local politicians are among those who would be pleased to provide you with speech material. Keep in mind, though, that no matter how expert the person you are interviewing, you don't want to overload your speech with references to that interview. Unless you are an experienced note taker, you will want a recorder for your interview. Many smart phones now have the ability to record voice and there are many free Apps available for all smart phones for voice recording. Most subjects will gladly give you permission to record them if you explain exactly how you want to use the material.

You can also interview people electronically using services such as Skype. Add to the credibility of your speech with a statement supporting your plea for higher emission standards from a world-renowned environmentalist. Support your call for National Health Insurance with statements from Norwegian citizens who have had socialized medicine in their country for more than 92 years.

Finally, you can engage in an e-mail interview to gather information from an expert in a particular area. A speech student at a college in Wisconsin recently interviewed a representative of the United Farm Workers of America on the plight of farm workers and their families after a citrus freeze in California. The interview provided a poignant, firsthand look at the plight of thousands of migrant farm workers who were left homeless and starving. You can locate experts on the Internet utilizing LinkedIn, Twitter, or general Internet searches.

TAKING NOTES

The more accurate your notes are, the less time you will have to spend rechecking your sources for dates, statistics, and exact wording.

Although many students want to gravitate to taking notes with a laptop, tablet, etc., I find that the use of 3×5 note cards is still superior. There are a number of reasons for this: (1) Note cards are easy to handle. If a note card contains information that you decide not to use, you can throw it away. (2) Note cards can be shuffled and used to organize the speech. (3) Note cards can easily be used for reference during the delivery of the speech or during the question-and-answer period following it. (4) Note cards can more easily be grouped and classified. Here are some suggestions to follow when taking your notes:

1. Use uniform note cards. Whether you buy them or make them yourself, note cards that are uniform in size and stiffness are easier to work with and store.
2. Record the exact source of your information. When the source is written, indicate the call number, author(s), title, date, publisher, and page numbers in case you want to refer to the source again. If your information came from an interview, indicate the time and date of the interview along with the interviewed person's name and credentials.
3. Keep notes brief. Don't copy large selections of material at random. Be selective. Spend time deciding exactly what you want to say before writing.
4. Be accurate. If you are copying a direct quotation, make sure that the wording is exact. If you are paraphrasing, make sure the paraphrase accurately conveys the meaning of the original.
5. Indicate the subject of each note card. Then when you are ready to organize your speech, you can put the cards in piles according to the points they are supporting.
6. Take an ample number of notes. Don't be afraid of gathering too much information. It is much easier to select the best from an overabundance of information than to find you are short and have to go back and look for more.

If you do pursue electronic note taking, I recommend investigating new software such as OneNote, Notebook, and Together that have evolved and developed the ability to organize your ideas more succinctly in the digital realm. Remember, regardless of the innovation, many technologically savvy individuals still find tangible note cards easier for speaking notes.

Bibliography

It is sometimes necessary to include a bibliography with your speech outline to document the sources of your supporting material. A bibliography should be arranged alphabetically by the author's last name or the first important word in the title. When including a bibliography, type the first line flush with the left margin and indent subsequent lines. Use the samples below as models:

AN ARTICLE IN A PERIODICAL

"Withdrawal symptoms." J. Weber Jr. Business Week, pp. 20–1 Ag 2 '93.
"Clues in the brain (role of messolimbic dopamine system in drug and alcohol
   addiction)."
B. Came. Maclean's v106, pp. 40–1 J1 19 '93.

A BOOK

Koch, Arthur & Schmitt, Jason, *Speaking with a Purpose*, 9th ed. Pearson Education, Inc.

One advantage of using electronic resources when gathering supporting materials for your speech is that if you use a computer connected to a printer or access the information from your personal computer, you can record the information you need with the press of a button.

A WEBSITE

Tesla Motorcar Company. 2013. "Tesla Model S Electric Car." Web. 27 January. 2013.
   <http://www.teslamotors.com/>.

DISCUSSION QUESTIONS

1. Discuss how you keep track of the information you find online when you conduct research.
2. Discuss some material that would not be available/accessible online that might benefit a presentation.
3. What support material have you witnessed that worked well for speeches/presentations? What material has not worked well?

EXERCISES

1. Conduct a Boolean search and document how many hits come back as you add criteria and specifics. Can you get your search down to a couple thousand hits?
2. Set up and conduct an interview for your next classroom speech. Evaluate the interview and refer to your notes. How successful were you in gathering the information that you needed? Did you find the interview a useful source of information? Explain.
3. Individually brainstorm a list of topics that would be of interest to your classroom audience. After completing a list of 15 topics, compare your topics with a partner. Were there similarities?

6 Supporting Your Ideas

One of the best ways to improve your effectiveness as a speaker is to learn how to select and use supporting materials. Supporting materials are necessary to make your ideas clear or more persuasive to your listener. Although there are different lists of supporting materials, most experts in the speech field agree on these six: examples, explanation, statistics, testimony, comparison and contrast, and visual aids. You have most likely used each of these during your lifetime, perhaps without being aware that there was a specific name for each. Suppose, for example, that you want to convince your parents that your new boyfriend is the ideal male. You might use any of the six supporting devices to support your assertion:

Example: "Mom and Dad, you're going to love Chris. He's one of the kindest people I've ever met. He puts in 8 hr of volunteer work a week at the Mayville Nursing Home, he's a big brother to an 11-year-old boy from the inner city, and he supports a little Cambodian child through the Christian Children's Fund."

Explanation: "I see Chris as the perfect male. The consideration with which he treats me makes me feel special and loved, and his sensitivity to music, art, literature, and nature makes him a fascinating person to be with."

Statistics: "Chris is six feet tall, he weighs 180 pounds, and he makes over $60,000 a year."

Testimony: "Rabbi Silberg, who is on the board of directors of Mayville Nursing Home, says Chris is one of the hardest-working and best-liked volunteers they have."

Comparison and Contrast: "Chris isn't like any man I've ever met. The others have been interested in doing only what they want and in satisfying their own egos. Chris believes that love is a sharing, and that's the way he acts."

Visual Aids: "Here are some snapshots of Chris. Doesn't he have a pleasant, open face? And did you notice how neatly he dresses?"

EXAMPLES

When wisely chosen, the example is without a doubt the most effective and versatile of all the supporting devices. It may be a good idea to use at least one example as a support for every main point in your speech. Examples can be brief or detailed, factual or hypothetical, and humorous or serious. If an example is factual and familiar to your audience, you need only to cite it briefly since they know the details. If the example is hypothetical or unfamiliar to your audience, you must develop it in enough detail so that the point your story makes is clear to them. For instance, if you are talking about the problem of child abuse, and a highly publicized case has recently occurred in your community, you need only to mention the case briefly but clearly. If, however, the instance of abuse occurred in a different location or a number of years earlier, you might have to tell it as a short story with facts, names, and dates. Detailed examples are often called *illustrations*. These illustrations or stories can take the form of anecdotes, personal experiences, allegories, or parables. Using illustrations in your speech can provide your audience with clear mental pictures of particular instances or events.

When selecting supporting materials for your speech, look for appropriate and interesting examples that are clear, concise, and to the point. Note how the following examples support the speaker's central idea: Every adult American should have an up-to-date will.

Brief Factual Example

Although a will can be made out by an individual or for as little as $100 by a lawyer, over 50% of all Americans die without ever having made one. No doubt many of them planned to, but just put it off. For example, Supreme Court Justice Fred Vinson died without a will, and Senator Robert Kerr was in the process of writing one when he died unexpectedly.

Brief Hypothetical Example

There are many reasons for keeping your will up-to-date. Suppose that you name your sister as executor, and she dies, moves away, or is too ill to serve. What if federal or state laws or court interpretations of them change? Suppose that you move to a state where inheritance tax laws differ? All these are reasons for reviewing your will whenever major changes occur.

Detailed Factual Example

Uncle George died about a year ago. He had never made a will, and this created some real problems for his wife, Aunt Edna, and their three children, all minors. The checking and savings accounts were in my uncle's name and the bank wouldn't let Aunt Edna draw out any money. Because the deed for their house listed them as "tenants in common," the children were due to inherit two-thirds of the house. The result of this was that nobody would lend Aunt Edna money for a second mortgage on the house, and she could not sell it because, as minors, the children couldn't "sign off" ownership in favor of their mother. The whole matter had to be taken to probate court, where it still is. To date, Aunt Edna has yet to see a single penny of Uncle George's estate and has borrowed over $10,000 from her relatives.

Detailed Hypothetical Example

John Jones, a widower with four children, remarries. He registers everything he owns in joint ownership with the new Mrs. Jones knowing that she will provide for the children if he dies. A year later both are killed in an auto accident. To compound the tragedy, Mrs. Jones survives her husband by 1 hr, and his assets revert to her as co-owner. Unfortunately, Mrs. Jones had not made out a will, and the entire estate goes by law to her only blood relative, a cousin she doesn't even like. Because there was no will, none of Mr. Jones's assets went to his children, since Mrs. Jones was related to them only as a stepmother.

EXPLANATION

The purpose of explanation is to make an idea clear or understandable. Hence when someone asks "explain to me why you want to go to the store," the answer involves additional information to help justify the request. Obviously then, explanations are about elaborating on your reasoning and represent an excellent supporting device. Explanation can involve a number of different forms. It can include exposition, analysis, definition, and description.

Exposition

Exposition may be defined as a communication that gives information to your listeners in order to increase their knowledge or their understanding of a situation or process. A speech on how to use a fly rod, bake a cake, lower a ceiling, or make a fortune in the stock market will in each case employ exposition. When a gas station attendant gives you directions on how to get to a nearby city, and you in turn pass his explanation on to the driver of the car you are traveling in, both conversations have largely involved exposition.

Analysis

Analysis is the process of explaining something by breaking it down into its parts and examining them. You use analysis when you explain how something works. If, for example, you want to convince your listeners to install inexpensive, homemade burglar alarm systems in their cars, you would have to give them a clear idea of what is involved in this system and how it would work.

Definition

When you use a term or concept that is unfamiliar to your audience, you must define it either in your own words or in the words of someone else. Be careful not to use words in your definition that are more difficult to understand than the term or concept you are defining. For the sake of imaginativeness and interest, avoid using dictionary or Wikipedia definitions. They are often overly formal and complex. Keep your definitions clear and to the point, using wording that your listeners can readily understand.

Description

Description makes use of the five sensory appeals (the five senses being taste, hearing, sight, touch, and smell) to make clear to your listener exactly what is being communicated. Although it isn't necessary to appeal to all five in each communication, the more of them to which you appeal, the more effective the communication will be. Effective description can create images or word pictures in the minds of your listeners.

STATISTICS

When used correctly, statistics can be an effective means of support. However, unless your statistics are both valid and reliable, they should not be used.

It was Benjamin Disraeli who said, "There are three kinds of lies: lies, damned lies, and statistics." His comment points up the fact that statistics can often be manipulated to support almost any assertion. For this reason, it is wise to document the statistics you are using. This means indicating when and by whom the statistics were compiled. It is quite likely that there are those in your audience who have in the past been deceived by statistics. Put them at ease by using statistics that are up-to-date and compiled by a reputable source.

Try to make the statistics you use as interesting and uncomplicated as possible. Remember, it is your job as the speaker to maintain your listener's attention. Here are some suggestions to follow when using statistics.

Dramatize Your Statistics

If you can present your statistics in a dramatic or vivid way, they are more likely to be understood and remembered by your audience. When stated unimaginatively, statistics can often be quite dry. When stated in terms that a listener can visualize, they can be quite thought provoking.

Round Off Your Statistics

Remember, unless you repeat your statistics, your listeners will hear them only once. For this reason, it is a good idea to round off complex numbers. Although it may be more exacting, instead of saying that the medium income of police officers in this city is $35,167, round it off to "around $35,000" or "slightly over $35,000."

Display Your Statistics Visually

Complex statistical data should be presented on charts, tables, graphs, or diagrams in order to help your audience grasp what is being presented.

TESTIMONY

We live in a complex age, an age of specialization. For this reason, it is often wise for nonexpert speakers to support their ideas with the testimony of experts. The testimony of an expert or authority on a particular subject carries the weight of that person's education and experience. Few of us would quarrel with an ophthalmologist who recommends that we switch to bifocals or an auto mechanic who tells us that we need a new water pump. Unless we questioned their honesty or competency, we would have no reason to doubt their judgment. Consequently, when you are delivering a speech, support your opinions, if need be, with the opinions of others more expert than you to add credibility to your presentation.

When supporting your point of view with the testimony of others, you can either quote them verbatim or paraphrase what they have said in your own words. The decision is up to you. There are, however, two instances when it is better to quote directly than to paraphrase: (1) when the person you are quoting has said it so well you cannot possibly say it better, and (2) where the testimony is controversial and you want your audience to hear it straight from the source. Otherwise, it is perfectly acceptable to state the testimony in your own words. When doing so, be careful to paraphrase the testimony of another both fairly and accurately. As a speaker, you have a responsibility to be honest and straightforward.

If the experts you are citing are likely to be unfamiliar to those in your audience, give facts about them that will establish their credibility. Your listeners will give more attention to what Dr. Carl J. George, chairman of the Department of Psychology at the University of Wisconsin and author of *Knowing Your Child*, has to say about teenage suicide than they will to what Carl J. George or even Dr. Carl J. George has to say.

Although it is often important that the authority you are citing is up-to-date, this is not always necessary. It can often be very effective to back up your point of view by citing an authority from the past that most of your audience respects. For example, a reference to the Bible or other holy books can often be quite effective. Dr. Martin Luther King, Jr., was known to often merge biblical quotations within his political messages.

The use of testimony as a support is often less effective when dealing with a controversial subject. Anyone who has had anything to do with debate is aware that when you are dealing with a controversial subject of significance, there is sure to be an unlimited number of experts who disagree with one another.

Provided you have some expertise in regard to your subject, one of the best forms of testimony you can use is your own personal experience. If you have some background or experience in regard to your subject that qualifies you as somewhat of an expert, mention it in the introduction to your speech. Let your listeners know immediately that you are backing up the information you are giving them with your own *expert* testimony. If you wait until the middle or end of your speech to tell them about your background, chances are that some in your audience will think, "I didn't know the speaker was an expert on the subject. I guess I should have listened more carefully."

COMPARISON AND CONTRAST

One of the basic principles of education is that the only way you can learn anything new is to be able to relate it to something you already know. Therefore, the best way to teach the unknown is to compare it to the known. This kind of comparison is called *figurative comparison* or *analogy*. It describes similarities between things that are otherwise different such as bargaining meeting to a barroom brawl and a major speech to a parachute jump without a parachute.

A literal comparison describes similarities between things that are physically alike. It can often give your listener a clear mental picture of what you are talking about. For instance, if you say that the new dean looks like a young Matt Damon or that a Trident submarine is half again as long as a football field, you are offering your listener a clear basis of comparison. Less visual examples would be comparisons between home ownership in the United States in 2008 and 2013, academic standards in private and public universities, and jazz versus rhythm and blues. Literal comparisons are often used to reinforce particular points of view. How many times have you heard or used an argument similar to the following: "Why can't I learn to drive? Sally already has her driver's license, and she's a year younger than I am"?

Comparing differences is often called *contrast*. When you compare high school and college, living at home or living on your own, and apples and oranges, you are emphasizing differences rather than similarities between like things. Consider the comment, "Boy, you kids nowadays get away with murder. When I was your age I wouldn't dream of doing that." You are backing up your point of view by emphasizing differences rather than similarities.

VISUAL AIDS

Often it is necessary to use visual aids when presenting your supporting material. Some material is almost impossible to present without using them. Try demonstrating how to make jewelry or successfully ice fish without the proper equipment. Try contrasting impressionism with surrealistic art without showing your audience examples of each. When used effectively, visual aids can be an effective means of reinforcing and clarifying your ideas. An audience will retain the information you give them longer if they are both told and shown something at the same time. The old adage "A picture is worth a thousand words" applies. Effectively used visual aids will enhance your audience's interest and understanding. Be aware, however, that the visual aid should only reinforce or clarify your material. Showing your audience a good video or website may hold their attention but would be ineffective unless it was made explicitly clear what was to be gained from the showing. The word *aid* means to help or assist. That is what your visual aid should do. Some often used visual aids are listed next:

The item itself

Charts, graphs, and diagrams

Pictures (tangible and digital)

Flyers, pamphlets, and handouts

Paintings and posters

Chalkboards and flip charts

Photographs and drawings

Audio/video

Yourself or a volunteer from the audience

Benefits of Visual Aids

Visual aids help an audience remember what you say. An audience is far more likely to remember information when they are both told and shown something at the same time. For example, after 72 hr, most people can only remember 10% of what they have seen, 20% of what they have heard, but almost 65% of what they have both seen and heard.

Visual aids increase understanding, engage the audience, and allow the speaker to cover topics or ideas that would be difficult to describe in words alone. Charts and graphs can make complex statistics and relationships easier for your audience to understand.

Visual aids add interest to your speech and help to hold the attention of your audience. When effectively chosen, visual aids provide creativeness and variety to your presentation. The use of color in your aids will help you get and hold attention.

Visual Aid Software

It is important that the speaker constructs the easiest and quickest display of digital images etc. to make the visual display seamless to the presentation. Practicing your speech at home may not seem like a significant bother to quickly pull up an e-mail, cut-and-paste a link, and wait for the page to load. However, under the stress of speaking, perhaps with nervous hands etc., it is a much superior method to have your images preplanned and setup. Many have had success by utilizing PowerPoint, not necessarily to display text, but rather to just display the pictures and brief video and allow easy switching in succession between slides.

Some speakers utilize small clips of streaming video from providers such as YouTube, Google Video, and Vimeo. However, it needs to be noted that streaming files are still not 100% fail-safe. Fluctuating Internet speeds often create buffering pauses (where the computer is reading the file and not playing the video) that can quickly derail a presentation. It may be a good idea, if possible, to have digital video possessed on a hard drive, thumb drive as a second method should Internet speeds not be sufficient.

Another recent software that has grown in popularity for the presentation of information is Prezi.com. Prezi is a free software that allows the images to be scattered in a fashion similar to a large map and then zooms in to the location specified. It has been my experience that Prezi works better for group presentations and lectures rather than speeches. And it should be noted that Prezi has a learning curve and requires a level of technical knowhow that can make some user's attempts less than perfect. PowerPoint seems to serve the average user more effectively, and the recent edition provides some remarkably professional features.

Specific Suggestions for Using Visual Aids

When used effectively, visual aids can be an excellent means of reinforcing or clarifying your ideas. If, however, the visual aid is used incorrectly, it can detract from rather than improve your speech. Here are some specific suggestions for using visual aids:

1. A visual aid must be large enough to be seen by the entire audience. If you are using a poster or chart, make sure that your lettering or drawings are dark or vivid enough so that those farthest away will get the information. Unless each member of your audience can see your visual aid clearly, don't use it.

2. Avoid visual aids that are overly complex. A complicated drawing or too many words or statistics will defeat your purpose. A listener must be able to grasp the meaning of your visual instantly.

3. Your visual aid should clarify or reinforce your point. Displaying a picture of yourself holding a string of bass during a demonstration on how to fillet fish might do something for your ego but will add nothing to your audience's understanding.

4. Make sure that you maintain good eye contact when referring to your visual aid. It is for the audience, not you, to look at. Besides, looking out at your audience will help you determine if you are displaying your visual aid in a way that can easily be seen by all.

5. Whenever possible, use poster board or a flip chart rather than a chalkboard during your presentation. If you must use a chalkboard, avoid turning your back to the audience for an extended period. Limit your use of the board to a simple drawing or a few words or phrases, or put what you need on the board before you begin the speech.

6. Keep your visual aid out of sight except when you are using it. Attention is intermittent. A person pays attention to something for a while, stops for a moment or so, and goes back to paying attention again. If you leave an interesting visual aid out to look at, chances are that some in your audience might find themselves paying attention to it rather than your speech.

7. Include your visual aid when practicing your speech. Become so familiar with your visual aid that you can refer to any part of it with little loss of eye contact. Know where your aids will be when you want them and where you will put them when they are not being used.

8. Never pass a visual aid around through the audience. If you do, you will lose the attention of at least three listeners—the one looking at the aid, the one who has just passed it on, and the one who will be getting it next. An exception would be if you were passing out an aid or handout to each member of your audience. There is less chance that this activity will be distracting if you pass the items out near the end of your speech, perhaps even at the conclusion.

9. Make sure that your visual aid does not take up too much time. Remember, you are using the visual aid to support a point you are making in your speech, not as a section of the speech itself. Running 3 min of a movie or slides during a 5-min speech is an overly long and inappropriate use of visual aids. On the other hand, make sure that everyone has enough time to see and understand your visual aid.

10. Do not let your visual aid interfere with the continuity of your speech. If, for example, you are going through the steps of mixing the ingredients of a cake or applying glaze to a ceramic during a speech to demonstrate, don't stop talking to your audience while doing so. Your visual aid must support what you are saying, not substitute for it.

11. Be prepared to deliver your speech without your visual aid. No matter how careful you are when preparing and practicing with your visual aid, something can go wrong. Knowing that you can deliver your speech even if your visual aid fails will give you a sense of confidence and allow you to be more relaxed. Keep in mind, furthermore, that the ability to deliver a speech effectively when your visual aid fails will win you the admiration and respect of your audience.

12. Avoid presenting too much material on a visual aid. An overly complex visual aid may be worse than none at all. A visual aid should be clear, concise, and instantly understandable.

13. Make sure you have brought with you all the necessary equipment for displaying your visual aid. You most likely want a tape if you choose to put the visual up on a chalkboard/wall. Think of all the variables for a seamless display.

DISCUSSION QUESTIONS

1. Discuss a leader your classmates would respect in the following fields: science, education, energy, medicine, law, football, baseball, and music.

2. Have you witnessed a visual aid that failed to work for the presenter? If so, please explain.

3. Why are statistics such useful support in a speech?

EXERCISES

1. Find an ad that combines two or more supporting devices to sell its products. Do the supporting devices seem accurate and objective? Comment on whether you think the ad is effective and why or why not.
2. Log on to the website TED.com and watch a presentation that interests you. What types of supporting materials were used? Did this material make a difference in your evaluation of the speech? Explain.
3. Write a brief paper on the advantages and disadvantages of digital/online visual aids as opposed to tangible visual aids.

7 Organizing the Body of Your Speech

For years the company FranklinCovey Planners has supplied executives and business leaders an indispensable product: the personal planner. In recent times, planners have partially gravitated into the digital realm, but regardless the function stays the same: to have your information, contacts, ideas, and dates clearly organized and accessible. Leaders have shown, perhaps from the success of FranklinCovey Corporation, just how important organization is.

Now that you have gathered the supporting materials, you are ready to begin preparing the body of your speech. Just like good leaders and their quest for organization, a well thought out and organized body of the speech will increase the audience's interest, understanding, and retention of your information. The body of the speech should be developed around your central idea statement, which is the controlling idea of the speech. In most cases, the central idea of a speech quite naturally breaks up into two or three main points. For example, consider a speech with the topic *Our Food Court*. In developing a speech about *Our Food Court*, which is a clean, inexpensive, good place to meet people, and so on, you could quite likely come up with the central idea, "Our college food court is an excellent place to eat." You might support it with these three main points: (1) the prices are reasonable, (2) the food is well prepared, and (3) the surroundings are neat and clean. The basic format for this speech would be as follows:

Introduction: The introduction of a speech should capture the audience's attention, give them a reason for listening, present the central idea of the speech—in this case, "Our college food court is an excellent place to eat"—indicate your qualifications for giving the speech, and preview the main points of the speech.

Body: First main point—the prices are reasonable (supporting material).

Second main point—the food is well prepared (supporting material).

Third main point—the surroundings are neat and clean (supporting material).

Conclusion: The conclusion of a speech should end with a summary of the main points, a restatement of the central idea, a question, and a memorable statement.

Although some central ideas can logically be broken down into five or more main points, it is advisable to limit your speech to no more than four. Keep in mind that you are speaking to listeners who have to remember the information you are giving them. Few, if any, will be taking notes. If you have too many points, the chances are great that you will wind up confusing and perhaps even losing some of your audience.

ORGANIZING YOUR SPEECH

Introduction

An introduction should capture the attention of the audience, give them a reason for listening, present the central idea, indicate your qualifications, and preview the main ideas to be given. As a rule of thumb, the introduction should comprise 10% to 15% of the total speech time and should lead smoothly into the body of the speech.

Body

The body should comprise 75% to 85% of the speech. That is where the speaker's message is presented. The body consists of the main points of the speech, along with the supporting materials necessary to develop each point, and clear transitions from each point to the next.

Conclusion

A conclusion should be short and to the point. It should comprise 5% to 10% of the total speech and include one or any combination of the following: a summary of the main points, a restatement of the central idea, a question, a call to action, a vision of the future, and so on.

PLANNING THE BODY

The body is the most important part of the speech. It contains the development of the central idea, the major points, and the supporting material that proves or clarifies the central idea and main points. Therefore, it is wise to develop the body of the speech first. Since the body of the speech requires the most in-depth information, you will spend the majority of your time on this section of your speech. Keep in mind as you conduct your research that you are also looking for interesting concepts for the introduction and conclusion; if you come across items of interest, set them aside or bookmark them. To be successful in your construction of the body of the speech, follow these four steps:

1. Decide on the main points that will support or clarify your central idea.
2. Write these main points as complete sentences.
3. Arrange the central idea and main points in a logical organizational pattern.
4. Add appropriate supporting material to clarify and reinforce your central idea and main points.

Deciding on Main Points

The central idea statement you have chosen should determine the main points you select. The number of main points you need to put your ideas across is up to you, but two to four main points is usually an appropriate amount. Keep in mind during this stage that you are trying to get your audience to accept and remember your ideas. As I pointed out earlier, if you develop any more than four main points, chances are that some of your audience will be unable to remember them.

Write Your Main Points as Complete Sentences

Writing your main points as complete sentences will help you determine whether they reinforce or clarify your central ideas effectively and whether they cover your subject adequately. Each main point should be stated clearly and succinctly so that there is no doubt in your listeners' minds as to what your point is and what you are trying to accomplish. The following are four suggestions for developing main points for your speech:

1. They should clarify or reinforce your central idea.
2. They should cover your subject adequately.
3. They should be equal in importance.
4. They should be worded in a similar way.

THEY SHOULD CLARIFY OR REINFORCE YOUR CENTRAL IDEA   In order to be effective, your main points must make your central idea clearer or more forceful. These main points will in turn be clarified or reinforced by your supporting materials: examples, illustrations, statistics, explanation, testimony, comparison and contrast, and visual aids. Main points that do not clearly reinforce or clarify your central idea are confusing. Consider the following example:

Central idea: Iguanas make great pets.

Main point: They are inexpensive.

Main point: They are clean.

Main point: They are easy to care for.

Main point: They are reptiles.

Note that while the first three main points reinforce the central idea that iguanas make great pets, the fourth point, that they are reptiles, does not. While it can be argued that many reptiles make excellent pets, most would agree that others, like cobras or crocodiles, do not. The speech would flow much better without the "they are reptiles" main point.

THEY SHOULD COVER YOUR SUBJECT ADEQUATELY   In order to achieve your purpose in speaking, you must be sure to provide your listeners with the information they need to respond correctly. Choose your main points carefully so that they fully develop your central idea. It is always better to have too much material than to fail to cover a subject adequately. Remember, your success or failure as a speaker is largely dependent on audience response.

THEY SHOULD BE SIMILAR IN IMPORTANCE AND PARALLEL IN PHRASING Besides reinforcing and clarifying your central idea, your main points should be similar in importance to each other. Supporting your central idea with two strong points and one weak one will lessen the effectiveness. Also, wording your main points in a parallel manner will emphasize the fact that they are coordinated. One way to achieve parallelism of main points is to repeat key words. Compare these two sets of main points for a speech on swimming:

Nonparallel

Central idea: Swimming is beneficial to your health.

Main point: It conditions your mind and your body.

Main point: You exercise most of your muscles.

Main point: The capacity of your lungs is increased.

Parallel

Central idea: Swimming is beneficial to your health.

Main point: It conditions your mind and your body.

Main point: It exercises most of your muscles.

Main point: It increases your lung capacity.

Although the above changes are subtle, the results are powerful. The nonparallel phrasing above, jumping from "it" to "you" to "the," makes the focus unclear. Inversely, the parallel phrasing, always using "it," keeps a nice and easy to understand repetition of concepts.

The information that you are presenting to your audience must be organized in such a way that it makes sense and can be easily followed. The movie *What About Bob* starring Bill Murray emphasized the need to take "baby steps," and the fact that small steps add up. Try to make "baby steps" in your speech progression so as to not lose your audience.

Arranging the Central Idea and Main Points

You can organize the central idea and main points that you present in your speech in a number of ways. The seven most basic organizational patterns follow:

1. *General to Specific.* In a sense, a general-to-specific pattern is found in most speeches. The central idea, usually given in the introduction, is a general statement, and it is followed by a statement of the main points in less general terms. Finally, each of these main points is supported by specific details.

    Central idea: Betty White is an excellent speech teacher.
    Main Points:
    a. She has established an excellent rapport with her students and made them enthusiastic about speech.
    b. She has demonstrated her thorough knowledge of the subject along with sound teaching techniques.
    c. She has been able to communicate her understanding of speech to the students and has helped them improve.

2. *Chronological Order.* Many speeches lend themselves to development in a chronological order, especially informative speeches. In this pattern, you relate a series of incidents or explain a process according to the order in which the incidents or steps in the process occur or have occurred—from first to last. You might analyze the development of rock and roll or demonstrate how to make lasagna.

    Central idea: You must follow four steps when making lasagna.
    Main Points:
    a. Step 1 involves preparing the meat sauce.
    b. Step 2 includes making and cooking the pasta.
    c. Step 3 involves preparing the three cheeses.
    d. Step 4 is layering the ingredients into baking dishes and baking the lasagna.

3. *Topical.* Sometimes a pattern of arrangement is suggested by the topic itself. For instance, a discussion of music history might logically divide itself into four areas: preclassical, classical, romantic, and contemporary. Similarly, a discussion of a college or university might involve the board of directors, the administration, the faculty, and the student body. The method of topical order fits nearly every kind of speech, and due to its broad use, it is the most utilized speech organization method.

    Central idea: The development of music can be roughly divided into four broad areas.
    Main Points:
    a. The first is preclassical.
    b. The second is classical.
    c. The third is romantic.
    d. The fourth is contemporary.

4. *Spatial Order.* A subject might fall quite naturally into a spatial arrangement. An analysis of education in different parts of the country, a demonstration on how to landscape the front of a house, and an explanation

of how the body digests food would lend themselves to this pattern of development. Like the chronological order, spatial order is most used for informative speeches.

Central idea: Digestion, the process by which the body absorbs food, takes place in three areas of the body.

Main Points:

a. Digestion begins in the mouth, where the food is ground into a semisolid mass.

b. Digestion in the stomach, where food becomes a mixed liquid.

c. Digestion ends in the small intestines, where the final stage occurs.

5. *Cause and Effect.* Causal and effect is most often used for persuasive speeches although it can be used in informative contexts. It generally takes the form of two main points—one addressing the cause, the second dealing with the effects. A typical example is that of a salesperson trying to convince a prospective customer that buying the product (cause) will result in all sorts of advantages (effect). Following is an outline of a student speech that utilizes the cause-and-effect pattern to describe the negatives toward automobile pollution.

Central idea: Automobiles are polluting our air.

Main Points:

a. Vehicle pollution has a significant impact on our air quality.

b. If the problem goes untreated, we will have significant problems with the environment.

6. *Problem–Solution.* Another organizational pattern most often employed in speeches to persuade is the problem–solution order. This speech usually begins with an introduction that states a problem as the central idea of the speech. The body of the speech is organized around the solution or solutions to the problem. Following is a sample outline of a typical problem–solution speech.

Central idea: Because our student government has less funding, external fund-raisers are needed.

Main Points:

a. The amount of money that our student government will receive from outside sources this year has been cut in half, eliminating funding for many of our programs.

b. The solution to this problem is to hold a 2 day bratwurst festival during the month of October, which will raise enough money to make up the difference.

7. *Motivated Sequence.* Monroe's motivated sequence is yet another organizational pattern. It was developed in the 1930s by the late Alan H. Monroe, a speech professor at Purdue University. It lists a five-step plan of action.[*]

a. Capture the attention of the audience.

b. Indicate a need for the audience to listen.

---

[*]From Kathleen German, Bruce Gronbeck, Douglas Ehringer, and Alan Monroe, *Principles of Public Speaking*, 18th ed. (Boston, MA: Pearson, 2013), p. 222–226.

    c. Show how your proposal will satisfy that need.
    d. Visualize what will happen if the plan is put into operation.
    e. Indicate the action you wish your audience to take.
       Example. *Central idea:* Congress must pass a federal law requiring stiffer penalties for drunken driving.
      a. Show pictures of fatal crashes involving drunk drivers.
      b. Cite statistics that emphasize the problem.
      c. Show how tougher laws have worked in other countries.
      d. Describe life without the menace of the drunken driver on the road.
      e. Tell those in your audience to sign your petition.

Speeches that are well organized are clearer and therefore more effective. Using one of the organizational patterns given above will make it easier for those in your audience to understand and remember the information in your speech. You have undoubtedly come in contact with many of these organizational patterns before. That is because the mind is conditioned to organize chronologically, spatially, topically, logically, and from general to specific. Your chances of communicating effectively with your audience will be much greater if you use an organizational pattern that can easily be followed.

Add Appropriate Supporting Material

Supporting materials are necessary for clarifying or proving the points you make in the body of your speech. By themselves the major points are the only structure or skeleton of your speech. It is the quality and relevancy of the support material you choose that make your ideas clear, interesting, and acceptable to your audience.

Outlining Your Speech

An outline will help you get an overall feel for how your speech will progress. It will allow you to see how each section of your speech relates to others. An outline should be framed around a central idea statement. This should be a thesis statement—a statement of the main idea you are attempting to develop in your speech.

Although outlining your speech involves extra work, the rewards will pay off in dividends. The major benefit of an outline is that it allows you to check your speech for potential mistakes. A speech outline is essentially a plan of what you want to say. Carefully examining your outline will help ensure that the main points of your speech clarify or reinforce your central idea, cover your subject adequately, are equal in importance, and are worded in a similar way. In addition, an outline will enable you to assess whether your subpoints and supporting materials are adequate and sufficiently varied and whether your introduction and conclusion are appropriate to the body of your speech. Finally, an outline will help you determine where transitions might be needed. There are two types of outlines that may be helpful for developing and delivering your speech: (1) a planning outline and (2) a delivery outline. This section will deal with the planning outline from which a delivery outline, as given in Chapter 8, can be developed.

Planning Outline

Keep in mind, what you put down in a planning outline is only tentative. It can always be changed. You can't expect to come up with a finished product on your first try. You will probably wind up with a number of rough drafts before you decide on one you like. When your outline is complete, you will have the skeleton for your speech. The following guidelines will be helpful when developing a planning outline.

- Divide outline into three parts.
- Use standard outline form.
- Write out your main points.
- Support each main point.
- Develop your conclusion.
- Develop your introduction.
- Add transitions.

DIVIDE OUTLINE INTO THREE PARTS: INTRODUCTION, BODY, AND CONCLUSION A speech should be divided into three parts: the introduction, the body, and the conclusion. Each of these three parts has a specific function. The introduction should get your audience's attention, give them a reason for listening, indicate your central idea and qualifications, and preview your subject. The body should communicate your ideas clearly and meaningfully, and the conclusion should restate your central ideas and main points and tie them together in a neat package. "In other words," as someone wise once said, "in your intro, you tell the people what you're going to tell 'em; in the body, you tell 'em what you said you'd tell 'em, and in the conclusion, you tell 'em what you've told 'em." As basic as the prior seems, that is the exact form that works for communicating clearly in life.

USE STANDARD OUTLINE FORM Standard outline form requires that you write your outline in complete sentences and follow the rules of coordination and subordination. Coordination means that all statements at the same level in your outline are equal in importance. Subordination means that each statement in your outline supports the statement in the level directly above it.

Outline numbering follows this order:

I. Main Point Number 1 (Roman numerals)
  A. Supporting Point (Capital letter)
    1. Supporting Material (Arabic numeral)
      a. Evidence (small letter)
      b. Evidence
    2. Supporting Material
  B. Supporting Point
II. Main Point Number 2
    1. Supporting Material
      a. Evidence
      b. Evidence

Indent all headings in the outline. Place numbers and letters of all headings directly under the first word of the heading above. Roman numerals for main points are placed closest to the left margin. Note that the periods following the roman numerals line up directly below each other. Putting your ideas into this outline form allows you to see the relationship between main points, supporting points, subpoints, and supporting materials in your speech. Thus, you can judge whether main points are worded similarly and are approximately equal in importance; whether all points at a given level have about the same amount of support; and whether each level in the outline is related to the level above it.

WRITE OUT YOUR MAIN POINTS   The main points should be written as complete sentences and should clarify or reinforce your central idea. Combined, they should cover your subject adequately. They should be equal in importance and worded in a similar way. Your main points should be numbered in standard outline form. A speech with the central idea "Rocks Make Great Pets" might be supported with these four main points:

   I. They are inexpensive.
  II. They are easy to care for.
 III. They are fun to watch.
 IV. They are great to throw when you want to let off steam.

SUPPORT EACH MAIN POINT   Each main point in your speech requires specific supporting material. Supporting materials are necessary to make your ideas clear or convincing to your audience. As a rule of thumb, the more controversial your main point is, the more supporting material you will need to back it up. In any event, each main point should be supported by at least two supporting points. If you can't find at least two supports for a main point, it probably should be omitted. Supporting points should be supported by subpoints and so on.

Keep in mind that some speeches may have only one main point. A short speech to persuade with the central idea "Never buy anything sight unseen" might involve you telling your audience about an experience you had that taught a lesson that was the single main point of your speech: "I learned at an early age never to buy anything I hadn't seen first." You might deliver a speech of personal experience to entertain with a central idea that is also the main point: "Camping can be fun, for bears!"

DEVELOP YOUR CONCLUSION   A conclusion should be short and to the point. It should comprise 5% to 10% of the total speech and include one or any combination of the following: a summary of the main points, a restatement of the central idea, a question, a call to action, a vision of the future, and so on.

DEVELOP YOUR INTRODUCTION   The minimum purpose of any introduction should be to get the audience's attention and reveal your subject. However, most introductions should have five objectives: (1) to capture the audience's attention, (2) to present the central idea of the speech, (3) to indicate your qualifications for giving the speech, (4) to give the audience a reason for listening, and (5) to preview the ideas to be covered in the speech. As a rule of thumb, the introduction should comprise only 10% to 15% of the total speech time.

Following is an outline of the body of the speech whose central idea is "walking is the ideal exercise," to which supporting materials have been added.

Body of Speech

I. Walking strengthens the heart.
  A. Walking improves collateral circulation.
    1. (*Testimony*) Dr. Samuel Fox, president of the American College of Cardiology, says walking increases the number and size of your blood vessels and the efficiency of the heart.
    2. (*Example*) Steve McKanic was told at the age of 46 that his heart condition was incurable and that there was no hope. He started walking, and 5 years later, he's healthy and happy again.
    3. (*Statistic*) It is estimated that 12 million people in this country are being treated for heart disease that could be improved by walking and 12 million have heart disease but don't know it.
  B. Walking lowers blood pressure.
    1. (*Explanation visual aid*) Muscles in your feet, calves, thighs, buttocks, and abdomen help push 72,000 quarts of blood through your system every 24 hr. These muscles are exercised by walking, making them more efficient in lowering your blood pressure.
    2. (*Example*) Eula Weaver suffered her first high blood pressure heart attack at the age of 78. Today at 89, she walks regularly and her blood pressure is normal.
    3. (*Testimony*) A recent study by Dr. Kenneth Cooper, author of *Aerobics*, demonstrates the relationship between walking and a person's fitness level.
II. Walking conditions a person mentally.
  A. Walking reduces stress.
    1. (*Testimony*) Dr. Herbert DeVries, University of California physiologist, stated that a university study showed that a 15 min walk reduced neurotransmitter tension more effectively than a standard dose of tranquilizers.
    2. (*Example*) Albert Einstein, Harry Truman, and Abraham Lincoln walked daily to escape from the tension of their jobs.
    3. (*Testimony*) Dr. Paul D. White, dean of American cardiologists, said a minimum of an hour a day of fast walking is absolutely necessary for one's optimum health.
  B. Walking improves self-image.
    1. (*Testimony*) "Walking," says psychologist John Martin, "helps you function more efficiently because you know you are doing things that are positive and constructive which give you satisfaction."
    2. (*Example*) Aunt Rose, who had tried to lose weight for years, began walking and in 6 months went from a size 22 to 14.
    3. (*Explanation*) Walking improves circulation, sending more oxygen to the brain and creating a euphoria that improves self-concept.

III. Walking conditions a person physically.
   A. Walking removes unwanted fat.
      1. (*Visual aid*) This chart indicates the number of calories a person of particular weight will expend each hour by walking at various speeds.
      2. (*Statistical testimony*) Dr. Charles Kunzleman, national fitness consultant for the YMCA, estimates that there are presently over 60 million Americans who are seriously obese.
      3. (*Example*) Three-hundred-pound Molly Ryan, who felt her glandular problem kept her fat, began walking after a heart attack and lost 100 pounds the first year.
   B. Walking improves a person's fitness.
      1. (*Comparison*) A study of the health records of 30,000 double-decker bus workers in London found that the fare collectors who climbed the stairs regularly had a much lower mortality rate and faster recovery from heart attacks than the inactive bus drivers.
      2. (*Example*) Scrambling over the slopes of their mountainous homeland has given the long-lived citizens of Hunza in the Himalayas such a high degree of physical fitness that even when they suffer a heart attack it does little harm.
      3. (*Testimony*) Dr. Lawrence Golding conducted a controlled experiment at Kent State University that showed that walking combined with dieting was far superior to dieting alone in improving physical fitness.

TRANSITIONS

We have all watched great movies that keep us glued to our seat. After the conclusion of the movie we ask ourselves, "Where did the last 2 hours go?" Since we were so captivated with the story, the time flew by. In contrast, we have also all experienced less than perfect movies that often have us questioning 10 minutes in "What is going on?" In other words, great movies are smooth. One plot line leads to the next effortlessly and enjoyably. In less stellar work, when the plot is jumpy and we say "we were just in London, how did it move to Johannesburg?" that is a cue that the plot and story line is not working together. Just like good movies, we want our speeches to be smooth, engaging, and enjoyable.

The body of the speech outlined above consists of main and supporting points, along with supporting material for each. However, in order to move your listeners smoothly from one point to the next, you must include transitions or links between each point. Transitions are guides for your listeners and make your speech smooth. They are a way to get them from one point to the next. When you use words like *also* and *in addition* you indicate that your thinking is moving forward. Words like *on the other hand* and *conversely* indicate a reversal of direction. Imagine the following situation: An instructor walks into a class and says to her students, "As you all know, you are scheduled to take your mid-semester exam in this course today. However . . ." The instructor pauses. An audible sigh of relief is heard throughout the room. The word *however* has caused the students to reverse their thinking. There will be no exam today.

Transitions will help to provide coherence to your speech so that your ideas flow smoothly from one point to the next. Following are a number of suggestions for providing coherence to your speech:

1. Use transitional words: also, again, as a result, besides, but, conversely, however, in addition, in contrast, likewise, moreover, nevertheless, similarly, then, therefore, thus, yet.
2. Use signposts "There are three main reasons: first . . . second . . . third . . . " "Point A is this: . . . "
3. Repeat key words. "Our nuclear buildup isn't defense. Our nuclear buildup is suicide."
4. Conclude your discussion of one point by introducing the next point. "This concludes the discussion of step two, stripping. Next we will consider step three, sanding."
5. Begin your discussion of a new point with a reference to the point you just finished discussing. "Now that we have finished our discussion of step three, sanding, we are ready to move on to step four, refinishing."

Keep in mind that as a speaker you are obliged to do whatever you can to make your ideas as clear and interesting to your listeners as possible. Using effective transitions in your speeches will help you achieve this goal.

DISCUSSION QUESTIONS

1. Why do you think it is important that presentations be organized clearly?
2. What do transitions do for our speech?
3. How many main points should make up our speeches?

EXERCISES

1. Write out a central idea statement and two or three main points for one or more of the following subjects.
   a. Restaurants
   b. Hobbies
   c. Sports
   d. Fitness
   e. Entertainment
   f. Politics
2. Using the brainstorming technique, select a topic and write at least six ideas related to that topic. Briefly write the main and supporting points and an overview for the introduction and conclusion.
3. With a group come up with the main points for a speech on air pollution in a cause-and-effect manner.

8 Delivering Your Speech

Once you have determined your purpose and subject, analyzed your audience, and developed the content of your speech, you have finished the hardest part of your job. However, all the work you have done was for one ultimate goal: to deliver a good speech. In public speaking, the delivery is where the rubber meets the road or where all your prior research and practice have the opportunity to make you, and your abilities, create great results. There are several different delivery styles you can choose from, depending on a number of variables such as the purpose of your speech, the subject, the occasion, and your audience. The manner in which you prepare your speech for delivery will depend on the type of delivery you choose. Impromptu speeches (those delivered on the spur of the moment) are either not prepared at all or prepared very hastily. Manuscript speeches are written out completely and read. Memorized speeches are usually written out first and then committed to memory and delivered. Extemporaneous speeches are carefully prepared but delivered from note cards. In most cases, the extemporaneous method provides spontaneity that will enable you to adapt your message to your audience while you are speaking to them and to modify it when necessary in response to their feedback. Let's consider these four methods of delivery in more detail.

IMPROMPTU SPEECHES

An impromptu speech is one that is developed on the spur of the moment. There are times in a boardroom, at a meeting, or when asked a question that we need to think quickly, without ample preparation. These occasions utilize our impromptu or unrehearsed answers. This style of speaking demands a great deal of the speaker since it seldom gives time for advanced thought or preparation. When delivering an impromptu speech, you have little time, if any, to analyze the subject, audience, or occasion. You must think on your feet to choose and organize your material. While this can impart spontaneity and directness to your delivery, it can also result in inappropriate statements, unexpressed thoughts, and repetitiveness. Consider your own experience. How many times have you looked back at a situation and thought, "Why didn't I say that?" or realized that you had put your foot in your mouth and said the wrong thing?

There are times, however, when you will deliver an impromptu speech. As that situation arises, consider the following advice: (1) keep your speech short and to the point; (2) try to use illustrations for supporting material (from personal experience if possible); (3) handle only one main point; and (4) make sure your central idea and purpose are absolutely clear to your audience.

MANUSCRIPT SPEECHES

A manuscript speech is one that is completely written out in advance. It is used in situations where the presentation must be very precise. You would probably choose a manuscript speech if you were reporting to a group on a convention that you attended as their delegate or explaining a complicated statistical procedure. While the manuscript speech offers security to speakers afraid that they will forget what they want to say or say it badly, it has a number of disadvantages: (1) it reduces eye contact with the audience; (2) reading a speech is often monotone; and (3) the speaker has difficulty in changing the language or content of a manuscript speech to adapt to the mood or reaction of the audience.

Even though you may be willing to accept these disadvantages in return for the security of a manuscript speech, the best advice is to deliver a manuscript speech only when time does not permit you to prepare and practice an extemporaneous speech or when exact word order is crucial to the success of the presentation. To deliver a manuscript speech effectively, consider the following suggestions.

1. Type your manuscript speech to ensure easy reading. Type on only one side of the paper and number the pages.
2. Edit your speech by reading each sentence aloud. Avoid overly long or complex sentences. No matter how involved or technical your material is, it must be communicated clearly.
3. Indicate places of emphasis and pauses (perhaps by highlighting them with a unique color).
4. Practice your manuscript by reading it aloud at least 3 or 4 times. Become familiar enough with it so that you can maintain adequate eye contact. You should sound as though you are talking to people, not reading to them.
5. Use appropriate facial expression and body action to energize your delivery.

MEMORIZED SPEECHES

A memorized speech is written out as a manuscript speech and then committed to memory. While it appears to offer the advantages of a manuscript speech along with total eye contact, it has a number of weaknesses: (1) it takes an inordinate amount of time to memorize a speech, particularly a long one; (2) it takes a skillful actor to deliver memorized material in a natural, spontaneous way; (3) the speaker who delivers a memorized speech runs the risk of forgetting; and (4) as with the manuscript speech, it is difficult to change a memorized speech to adapt to feedback from the audience. However, for the right person, the memorized speech can be an excellent method, especially for someone who plans to give the same speech a number of times.

There are times when it would be desirable to commit part of a speech to memory. You might want to memorize the first few lines of the introduction to your extemporaneous speech in order to start positively and with total eye contact. Memorizing particularly suitable words or phrases can often produce positive results. Actually, most effective speakers use a combination of different delivery methods.

EXTEMPORANEOUS SPEECHES

Extemporaneous speeches are the most widely used speeches in public speaking. Like the manuscript and memorized speech, the extemporaneous speech is carefully prepared in advance. The difference is that the speaker does not deliver the speech in a predetermined word order. Effective extemporaneous speakers usually develop their speeches on note cards utilizing phrases and keywords as opposed to long sentences. In extemporaneous deliveries, the speaker knows what they are going to say in the introduction, body, and conclusion of the speech but decide on the exact wording of the speech at the moment of delivery. You might compare extemporaneous speech delivery with the telling of a funny story. Most people tell a funny story extemporaneously. They are aware of the important details of the story and know how the story is going to unfold, but they haven't memorized the word order. As long as they include those details necessary to make the humor clear, they can tailor the story for any occasion The extemporaneous speaking style is both versatile and powerful. The spontaneous style of speaking maintains some written notes so as not to forget where your speech is progressing which is the main advantage of extemporaneous delivery.

NONVERBAL COMMUNICATION

A great deal of what we communicate to others is communicated nonverbally, through our bodily movement, facial expression, personal appearance, voice, and so on. Obviously, it is important that these nonverbals reinforce the words that we use when communicating something to others.

Have you ever had a person tell you something when you could tell by her tone of voice, gesture, or facial expression that she did not mean what she said or meant just the opposite? We say a great deal to others by the way we look and sound when we say it. In fact, most listeners will give more credence to what we say nonverbally than what we say verbally.

Given the importance of nonverbal communication in delivering the speech, it should be a prime consideration when constructing a speech. In the broadest sense, nonverbal communication includes almost everything about you that communicates something to others except for the language you use. This would include the car you drive, the clothes you wear, your hairstyle, the organizations you belong to, the friends you associate with, and whatever else there is about you that communicates who you are and what you stand for. However, we are going to focus on the most important components of nonverbal communication for public speaking: the speaker's body and the speaker's voice.

The Speaker's Body

The way you walk, your manner of gesturing, your posture, your facial expression, and the way you look at people or avoid looking at them, all say something about you to others. Kinesics is the study of how the body, face, and eyes communicate. Whether they are interpreted by others correctly or incorrectly, these nonverbal elements communicate to others who you are.

BODILY MOVEMENT Consider the speaker who can't stand still, who paces back and forth in front of the audience. Does that speaker seem to be communicating nervousness? Or, consider the speaker who shuffles slowly up to the front of the room and leans over the podium when delivering the speech. Does that speaker's movement indicate weakness in confidence or preparation? On the other hand, consider the speaker who strides briskly up to the front of the room and stands in front of the audience with good posture. Isn't that speaker saying, "Pay attention. I've got something to say to you that you will find interesting"? These examples show the importance of positive bodily movement. It is all right to move around occasionally as long as the movement seems motivated by what you are saying. You might move to indicate the beginning of a new idea or a change of direction in your speech. You might move closer to an audience to share something personal or indicate a positive feeling toward your audience. The key is that your movement should seem motivated by what you are saying and not detract from it.

Your listeners begin forming opinions of you the moment they see you. Therefore, when you go up to deliver your speech, walk up to the podium briskly with a friendly expression on your face. Then, when you finish your speech, smile at the audience (when appropriate) and return to your seat as briskly and enthusiastically as you came.

The bodily movements of your listeners can also be helpful in predicting how well you are doing in communicating. The speaker who sees audience members leaning forward in their seats knows she is doing a good job. Feedback is highly important to the communicator. You don't have to have people turn their backs to know they are not interested in what you're saying. If they lower their heads or shrug their shoulders, you soon get the idea, and if you can react to these signals and say it in another way, you will have become more aware of nonverbal audience feedback, which will improve your ability to communicate.

Another kind of bodily movement is the gesture. You can gesture with almost any part of the body. A shrug of the shoulders can communicate many things, depending on the situation. A shake of the head can indicate agreement or disagreement, depending on the direction. Toe tapping can indicate nervousness or irritation. On the other hand, when combined with music it can also indicate that the toe tapper is synchronized with the music. It is apparent, then, that most bodily gestures can communicate a variety of things and must be evaluated according to the situation.

Hand gestures are very important to the speaker. Hand gestures can be divided into two types: descriptive gestures and emphatic gestures.

Descriptive Gestures   If you are describing to your listeners how large the tomatoes you grew were or how high your fence is, you can use your hands to give them an idea of shape or height. You can also use your hands to describe a winding staircase, a circle, or a square.

Emphatic Gestures   Emphatic gestures emphasize what you are saying. The synchronized gestures of cheerleaders at a pep rally emphasize the importance of the team getting out there and winning. Emphatic gestures are nonverbal messages that support our concern or enthusiasm for our message. When we fail to reinforce our words with appropriate gestures, we risk sending a confusing message to those with whom we are trying to communicate.

THE FACE AND EYES   One reason to avoid manuscript speeches or any speech where you are too dependent on your notes is to avoid obscuring your face and eyes. If your head is bent forward when you speak, your audience cannot see your eyes or read your facial expressions, which can communicate a wide range of emotions including sadness, compassion, concern, anger, annoyance, fear, joy, and happiness.

Maintaining eye contact with your audience is important for a number of reasons. First, you communicate to your audience both verbally and nonverbally. You say a great deal to them with your facial expressions, especially with your eyes. An audience will have difficulty seeing your facial expressions if you have your head buried in your notes.

Second, you indicate your interest in others by looking at them. It is a way of saying to each of them, "You are important." It is desirable to get each listener to feel that he or she is being addressed personally. Although you might not be able to look directly at each individual in a large group, be careful to focus on the eyes of as many individuals as possible in all parts of the room. Be sure to include those in the front and back rows and those on the extreme right and left.

Third, eye contact is often thought of as an indication of honesty and sincerity. If your parents asked you how things are going at school and you looked down or averted your eyes when you tell them things were great, would they be likely to believe you? Whether true or not, we often feel that if people don't look at us when they are telling us something important, they either have something to hide or are stretching the truth.

A final, very important reason for maintaining eye contact is to obtain feedback from the audience. We look at those to whom we are communicating in order to get their reactions to what we are saying. We can tell through changes in their facial expressions, postures, and gestures whether they are interested or bored, understanding or confused, supportive or opposed, and, hopefully, we react accordingly.

PERSONAL APPEARANCE The way you dress is often interpreted by others as communicating a great deal about who and what you are. Although perceptions based solely on personal appearance can often be wrong, personal appearance is still a powerful nonverbal communicator. When deciding what to wear, a good rule of thumb is to take your cue from your audience. People are most comfortable with those who dress the way they do. You should dress in something you feel comfortable wearing. Of course, you should dress for the occasion. When in doubt about what to wear, the safest thing to do is dress a bit more conservatively.

The Speaker's Voice

There are many ways that the voice can communicate. Vocal elements like rate, pause, volume, pitch, pronunciation, intensity, force, and vocal quality can either reinforce or contradict the verbal messages you are sending. Paralanguage refers to how you say something. Emphasizing different words within the same sentence can change the meaning of the sentence significantly. The tone of voice you use can communicate different types of emotions: anger, sadness, elation, boredom, sincerity, excitement, sarcasm, affection, fear, and so on. Like the other nonverbal elements listed above the voice of the speaker is of the utmost importance in communicating your meaning to others. In fact, when your voice contradicts the verbal message you are sending, most people are inclined to believe what the voice is communicating.

VOCAL ELEMENTS Effective communication employs many elements that lead to a strong speaking voice.

Rate Rate, the speed at which a person speaks, can vary depending on the situation and the emotional attitude of the speaker. The average speaking rate is between 125 and 150 words per minute. However, people who are excited, enthusiastic, or angry often speak at a much faster rate, whereas those who are lethargic, bored, or depressed speak more slowly. Because of the nonverbal connection between a faster rate and enthusiasm, announcers read hard-sell commercials considerably faster than 150 words per minute.

Pause Pause in speech can be either filled (vocalized) or unfilled (silent). A person who pauses continuously during a speech and who fills those pauses with *ahs* and *ums* is often thought of as being poorly prepared. Pause, however, can also be very effective. Dramatic pause, when used before an important point, can alert the listener to be especially attentive because something important is coming. When used at the end of an idea, it can give listeners time to think about what has been said and relate to the idea from their own experience. Effectively used, pause adds meaning and variety to a speaker's delivery.

Volume   An essential element to any communication is adequate volume—the loudness or softness of your voice. If people cannot hear you adequately, they will soon stop listening. One of the nonverbal aspects of volume is that it tends to communicate positiveness and confidence. If you ask two people the same question and one responded in a barely audible voice, while the other answered with sufficient volume, whom would you believe? Probably the second one who sounded both confident and positive—if, of course, that person did not speak too loudly. Adequate volume is essential to effective communication. However, most people view those who speak too loudly as being aggressive. Your volume will be effective if your voice can be easily heard without being offensive.

Pitch   Pitch refers to the highness or lowness of a person's voice as related to a musical scale. A natural conversational style is characterized by a variety of inflectional patterns. Inflection is understood when we look at the different ways "yeah" can be used. A "yeah!" after scoring the winning goal or the "yeah" you give when you are asked if you forgot to study for an exam show differing inflection. A voice without these inflectional patterns sounds monotonous and drastically loses its power to engage an audience. Nonverbally, upward inflectional patterns are thought to communicate enthusiasm, sincerity, and excitement while downward patterns communicate boredom, sarcasm, and dejection. To communicate enthusiasm and sincerity and to add interest to your speech, use a variety of inflectional patterns.

Quality   Your voice quality is determined by a number of things, some of which you cannot control. Two of these—timbre and resonance—are greatly influenced by the size and shape of your head and body. It is no accident that most famous opera singers have similar bodily features: wide cheekbones, large mouths, and ample lung capacity. These provide both timbre (the distinctive sound that characterizes one voice from another) and resonance (fullness and richness of sound) to their voices. However, that is not to say that without these bodily features you cannot make improvements in your vocal quality. Supporting your voice with deep full breaths of air and opening your mouth more full when speaking helps to create a more engaging voice for many speakers.

Articulation   Articulation is the process of forming the consonant and vowel sounds of words. These sounds are sculpted heavily from using the lips, teeth, and tongue to create distinctive sounding words. Improper articulation results in indistinct speech. If you articulate your words poorly, you will be difficult to understand.

The three most common errors in articulation are running words together, substituting one sound for another, and omitting necessary sounds. For example, *did you* becomes *di ja, student* becomes *stoont, asked* becomes *ast,* and so on. This kind of careless articulation is distracting to an audience. In order to deliver your speech effectively, you must make sure that your articulation is precise.

Pronunciation   While articulation is the process of forming the consonant and vowel sounds of words, pronunciation is much more complex. It involves articulating the correct consonant and vowel sounds of a word and accenting that word in a proper manner. Or put in simpler terms, pronunciation means saying a word the way it should be said. Owing to the makeup of the English language, that is not always an easy task. Several characteristics of our language make the task even harder.

There are an inordinate number of ways to pronounce the same vowel in our language. People who study English as a second language are often frustrated by the fact that the same vowel is often pronounced differently in different words. For example, consider the six pronunciations of the letter *o* for the following words: *do, no, dot, oar, woman,* and *women.* Even some words that are spelled alike can require different pronunciations depending on the form they take. For instance, the word *read* as in "Read the same passage you read yesterday."

EFFECTIVE WORD CHOICE

In order to deliver your speech effectively, you must use a language that is clear, interesting, and appropriate. An audience cannot respond to a message that is unclear to them, will not pay attention to a message that is uninteresting to them, and will reject a message they feel is inappropriate. Below are suggestions for making the language in your speech more effective.

Clarity

While clarity is important in all communication, it is indispensable to public speaking. A reader can reread a passage as many times as necessary to understand it. For the audience of a speech, it must be instantly understood or it is gone. If too much of what you say is missed or misinterpreted, your communication will fail. You can achieve clarity in speaking by choosing concrete rather than abstract words, and using specific rather than general words.

CONCRETE WORDS   Concrete words refer to specific objects or particular instances, things that are relatively easy to visualize or define. They differ from abstract words, which refer to concepts, ideas, or emotions and often mean different things to different people. *Dog, book, rose,* and *classroom* are concrete words. *Democracy, love,* and *hate* are abstract words. Obviously, a concrete word will always be clearer to your audience than an abstract one. Whenever possible, choose concrete rather than abstract words for your speech. When you must use abstract terms, define them as clearly and as completely as you can.

SPECIFIC WORDS   Another way to achieve clarity in your speaking is to choose specific rather than general words. General words refer to a group or class of things. Specific words refer to a particular part of that group. Specific words are always clearer. Imagine going to your favorite butcher shop and asking for two pounds of meat. How can the butcher fill your order without knowing what kind of meat you want? Two pounds of beef is better but still not specific enough. Do you want hamburger, ground chuck, rib roast, pot roast, or eye of round? Even if you say steak, you leave the butcher wondering which one of a dozen or more kinds of steak you mean. When wording your speech, do your audience and yourself a favor and be as specific as you can.

INTERESTINGNESS

An effective way to make your speeches more interesting is to use words that appeal to any of the five senses: sight, hearing, taste, touch, and smell. Engaging these senses creates great speeches and using this same philosophy has been the result of so many popular music hit songs. The songs, or speeches, that create the best images in the audience's head, are often the runaway successes. For example, while it might be perfectly accurate to tell your listeners that a man came toward you, it would be much more visual and therefore more interesting to them if you told them that he staggered, lurched, inched, or crawled toward you. In the same manner, the *eager buzz* of excited fans at a homecoming game and the spicy red chili that heats the mouth and causes perspiration to rise from the pores of the brow present vivid images to those listeners who can relate to them through one or more of their senses.

A second way of adding interest to your speeches is to use descriptive language to present a clear and definite word picture of what is taking place. Note the following two statements: (1) I sat next to a pretty blonde. (2) I sat next to a tall, slender, tanned blonde with a round and radiant face and dark, inviting eyes. Which statement is more likely to hold attention and establish a clear mental picture?

A third way to make your speeches interesting is to talk in terms of actual people and places. This technique involves giving names to the characters you describe in your stories. For example, it is easier to imagine yourself sitting next to *Sheldon* or *Juanita* than next to your *friend*. One can more easily picture you being attacked by the neighbor's vicious boxer, Cruncher, than by the "dog next door."

Finally, you can make your speeches interesting by using the active rather than the passive voice. An added benefit is that besides being more vigorous, the active voice is usually less wordy. Note the following examples:

Passive: *First, the water was boiled by Jane, and then the eggs were added.* (13 words)

Active: *Jane boiled the water first and then added the eggs.* (10 words)

Passive: *The rapist was shot by the intended victim.* (8 words)

Active: *The intended victim shot the rapist.* (6 words)

APPROPRIATENESS

When presenting your speech, you must be aware of using appropriate language for your audience and the occasion. It would obviously be inappropriate to use sophisticated scientific terminology in explaining the problems faced in rocket liftoff to a group of tourists. Not so obvious would be using electrical terms (even though simple) in a demonstration speech to a general audience on how to install a 220-V outlet. The terms would most likely be beyond the majority of the audiences understanding and would have to be described very clearly. Unless you know your audience extremely well and the occasion warrants it, it is best to avoid profanity. Always keep in mind that you are speaking to a captive general audience—not just your closest friends. While you might capture the attention of some in your audience with the startling use of a four-letter word, any advantage you gain will be negated if you make others uncomfortable or antagonized.

Finally, except in cases where you make it obvious that you are deviating for a special effect, always observe the rules of correct grammar. An audience will forgive or even miss an occasional slip, but if your speech contains too many errors, it will affect your credibility. Like it or not, one variable by which an audience tends to judge the competence of speakers is by their correct or incorrect use of language.

USING NOTE CARDS

Most effective speakers choose to deliver their speeches from note cards rather than from a delivery outline because note cards offer several advantages. Note cards are easier to handle than a sheet of paper and are less noticeable. They won't waver if your hand trembles slightly. Note cards are especially helpful if you must deliver your speech without a lectern because you can hold the cards in one hand and still be able to gesture freely. Here are a number of suggestions to follow when using note cards for an extemporaneous speech:

1. Use standard three-by-five-, four-by-six-, or five-by-eight-inch note cards. The number of cards you use will depend on the length and complexity of your speech. If you choose to make your own cards rather than buy them, use rigid paper or cardboard.
2. Use your note cards in a subtle way, staying as natural as possible, unless reading a direct quotation or complicated statistics. In these cases, hold your notes up so that your audience can see you are taking special care to be accurate.
3. Make sure your notes are legible. Note cards are easy to read when they are typed or printed in capital letters and double spaced and also work well if handwritten in neat legible printing.

4. Number multiple note cards. That way you will be able to put them in order quickly if you happen to drop them or find they are out of order.
5. Write on only one side of your note card. Even though your audience will expect you to use notes when delivering your speech, turning the cards over is distracting and time consuming.
6. Avoid writing your notes in too much detail. Note cards should serve only as a guide when delivering your speech. Overly detailed note cards make for too long of glances to capture the information off the card.
7. Avoid putting too much down on each card. Except for cards on which you have written full quotations or a set of statistics, limit the number of lines you put on a card. That way you'll be able to find your place in an instant. Remember, except for direct quotations and complicated statistics, the notes are there to jog your memory. Longer speeches will just require more cards.
8. Highlight ideas you wish to stress. Circle or underline key words so that you will remember to emphasize them while delivering your speech. It is often helpful to make notations on your note cards to *pause* or *slow down* at different times during your speech. Different colors of highlighting also help to direct you and your eyes to the right section for your quick glances.

When you deliver a speech in class, you are communicating in a friendly atmosphere. You are speaking to fellow students who can empathize with you because they are in the same situation as you are. Under these circumstances, a speaker should feel relaxed and at ease—but many don't. Why? Many beginning speakers see the situation as threatening rather than friendly. They worry that their classmates will see their shortcomings and imperfections, real or imaginary. Worrying too much about what other people will think of you can cause nervousness. This is not to say, however, that you should not be concerned with what your listeners will think of your speech. You have good reason to be nervous if you deliver a speech for which you have done little to prepare or practice. While most listeners will expect you to make mistakes while delivering your speech, especially if you are a beginning speaker, few will react favorably to your presentation if they feel it has involved little effort on your part. It is not hard to understand why those who are poorly prepared suffer from nervousness.

PRACTICING THE SPEECH

The key to delivering effective speeches is to practice heavily. Here are some suggestions for practicing your speeches:

1. Allow ample time for practice. Don't wait until the day before your presentation to finalize your speech and begin practicing.
2. Always practice with the same note cards that you plan to use when delivering your speech. If you rewrite something, run it through a practice session to make sure you haven't written in an error or left something out.

3. Always practice your speech as if you were delivering it to your intended audience. After you have practiced alone a few times, try to find a person or two to serve as your audience.
4. Practice your speech aloud with the same volume you plan to use in delivering it. Don't go over the speech in your head or say it so softly that no one can hear you.
5. Practice your speech each time with whatever visual aids you plan to use. If you plan to mix some ingredients together during your speech, mix them during at least one practice session. This will help prevent slipups.
6. Time your speech in practice. No one appreciates a speech that goes on and on interminably. If you have been given a specific time limit for your speech, conform to it while practicing. As a safeguard, arrange for a friend in the audience to signal you when you have only one minute or so left.
7. Practice the way you will approach the speaker's stand at the beginning of the speech and leave it at the conclusion.
8. Visualize giving your presentation successfully and remember how good it feels to succeed in front of an audience.

DELIVERY DISTRACTIONS

Slouching	Pulling on ear
Rigid posture	Rattling keys or coins in pocket
Clenching lectern	Adjusting glasses
Drumming fingers	Fluffing hair
Twisting ring	

DELIVERY PITFALLS

Here are some common pitfalls to delivery that you should avoid:

1. **Mispronunciation**—Make sure that you pronounce words correctly.
2. **Not being heard**—When you are competing with external noise or some other distraction make sure you speak loudly and clearly.
3. **Equipment not working**—Check your equipment. Avoid the embarrassment of equipment not working or your not being able to operate it.
4. **Conflicting messages**—A significant delivery pitfall occurs when your verbal message says one thing and your nonverbal says another; for example, saying to an audience "I'm really happy to be here!" when your posture, gestures, and facial expression are telling them that you're not. Remember, nonverbals communicate a great deal to the audience, and, in most cases, the audience will believe nonverbals over verbals.

5. **Ineffective gesturing**—If the gestures you use do not reinforce your message, they interfere with it. Don't plan gestures. They should be spontaneous.

6. **Uninteresting voice**—Enthusiasm and variety are important in maintaining your audience's attention.

7. **Poor eye contact**—Eye contact indicates honesty, sincerity, and interest to an audience. Avoid overdependence on your notes.

8. **Inappropriate humor**—If you are not positive the humor is appropriate, don't use it! Offensive or inappropriate humor can ruin your presentation.

9. **Ineffective transitions**—Without effective transitions in your speech, it will be hard for your audience to follow the movement from one idea to another.

10. **Weak introduction**—An effective introduction is imperative for gaining the audience's attention and letting them know what they're going to hear and why they should listen.

11. **Weak conclusion**—The conclusion is the last thing your audience hears. Some feel it is the most important part of the speech. An ineffective conclusion can spoil an otherwise good effort.

DISCUSSION QUESTIONS

1. What does nonverbal communication refer to?
2. What are the elements that make up a good speaking voice? What are some things we should be aware of when constructing a useful note card for speaking?

EXERCISES

1. Pay close attention to the conversations you have with your friends, family, teachers, and coworkers. Take note of the vocal elements in their conversation. Do they use fillers? Pause frequently? Do they articulate clearly and pronounce their words correctly? What other factors do you notice? Do these factors affect how well they communicate? Have you noticed these factors before?

2. Make two lists—one with concrete words and the other with abstract words. Choose several of the words and try to write down as many different meanings as you can. Is it easier to come up with meanings for the concrete words? Are the abstract words harder to define?

3. On YouTube.com find two speakers who you believe have strong vocal characteristics. After selecting the videos, write what specific traits of good speaking are present in your selected presentations.

9 Informing

We live in an increasingly complex age—one of new technology, endless research, and specialization. Each year, more and more new information is added to the total of human knowledge. There are currently more than 540,000 words in the English language, about 5x times as many as during Shakespeare's time. Combine the increasingly diverse word selections coupled with Google currently having more than 88 billion searches conducted on its service every month, and it becomes obvious we live in a world increasingly focused on information.

Our fascination as a society isn't just retrieving information, it is also conveying our information to others. According to Pew Internet, teens are sending roughly 75 text messages per day. Older girls are the most prolific communicators, sending an average of 100 text messages per day. Compare that number with boys, who sent about 50 messages per day.

All too often we take informative communication for granted. We watch YouTube videos, read our favorite blogs, and occasionally tune in for breaking news, yet we often aren't aware that information is the main ingredient for most of our activities. The better we become at delivering information to others, the more power, intrigue, attraction, income, and respect is to come our way. And in a world that privileges information more than any time period in history, understanding how to inform your audience is pivotal.

There are many different ways to categorize and deliver information. This chapter will deal with three of the most popular categories: demonstration speeches, description speeches, and explanation speeches.

DEMONSTRATION SPEECHES

The demonstration speech is designed to show your audience how to do something so that they will be able to do it on their own or have a better understanding of how it is done. You might deliver a demonstration speech to teach your audience how to make Swedish pancakes or to show them how various mathematical problems can be solved with a slide rule. As with most speeches, the key to delivering a demonstration speech successfully is effective audience analysis. You must ask the question "Who is my audience?" and "What response can I expect from my listeners?" These questions help you to tailor your message to meet your audience where they currently are. You could teach an audience to make Swedish pancakes in a reasonable amount of time; however, unless those in your audience are familiar with a slide rule, it seems unlikely that you could do much more than give them an understanding of how a slide rule can be used.

In order to show someone how to perform a card trick, prepare a salad, carve a turkey, or read palms, you will want to use the technique of demonstration. Demonstration speeches can involve audience participation, but it is not required. In demonstrating the card trick, for example, you might ask one or two members of the audience to try the trick to show how easily it can be learned. When demonstrating palm reading, you might have members of your audience read the lines and marks on their own palms to identify their life lines, their character, and so on. When members of your audience are observers rather than participants in your demonstration, you must be careful to present your material clearly and interestingly enough so that you achieve your purpose: audience understanding.

Following are examples of demonstration speeches:

Demonstrations to Teach	Demonstrations for Understanding
How to:	How:
wrap a gift	a parachute is packed
recognize cuts of beef	a head is shrunk
apply a tourniquet	belly dancing is done
remove a stain	a lute is played
make jewelry	a person is hypnotized
use a juicer	fires get started
ride a unicycle	an abacus is used
build a canoe	ballet is danced

DESCRIPTION SPEECHES

A second method of communicating information, description, engages the listeners' senses by creating a clear picture of what is being communicated. In a description speech you describe an object, person, place, event, or experience.

You might give your listeners information about an object's appearance, what it sounds like, what it tastes like, what it feels like, or what it smells like. You might describe a major event that you witnessed and what it felt like to be there.

Types of Description Speeches

Descriptions of people, places, and events are part of our everyday communication. We insist on an in-depth description of our roommate's cousin before agreeing to a blind date. We talk to a number of people who have vacationed at that new island paradise before we agree to go. We listen to a description of the events that took place at last year's homecoming game before buying our tickets for this year's game. Following are three types of descriptive speeches:

DESCRIBING A PLACE   A vivid description of your hometown or favorite place can make an effective speech. This can be a particularly effective presentation when the speaker is describing a location with which most of the audience is unfamiliar.

DESCRIBING AN EVENT   The description of an event can be an effective informatory speech. An eyewitness account of the Olympic Games, a rocket launching, a bank robbery, or other such topics could be developed into exciting, attention-holding presentations.

DESCRIBING HISTORICAL EVENTS   The historical events speech involves describing an episode or sequence of events in history. A vivid description of the scene, characters, and setting of the battle of the Alamo would effectively hold an audience's attention. Following are samples of historical events speeches:

The Battle of Bunker Hill	Custer's Last Stand
Watergate	September 11, 2001
D-Day	The Valentine's Day Massacre

EXPLANATION SPEECHES

The primary purpose of explanation is to make things clear or understandable. As a student, you are constantly involved with explanations. The school course catalog explains what courses your school offers and which ones you have to take to satisfy the requirements for your degree. Your instructors and advisors are primarily explainers. The syllabi you get at the beginning of the semester are explanations of what you will be studying in each course and what you are expected to accomplish.

Explanation speeches are those that explain a process, concept, idea, or belief. They include speeches to explain a process, to instruct, and to review.

SPEECHES TO EXPLAIN A PROCESS   Speeches to explain a process inform an audience how something works. While they are often organized similarly to demonstration speeches, they differ in purpose. A student of photography might deliver a demonstration speech on how to take an effective digital photograph. If he or she is asked to deliver an explain-a-process speech, an appropriate choice would be: how a digital camera works. Following are examples of explain-a-process speeches:

How:	
a generator works	an electric car operates
food is digested	a steam engine works
photosynthesis occurs	cell phones operate
the eye functions	kidneys clean your blood

SPEECHES TO INSTRUCT   Instructive speeches are presentations in which the speaker explains information about concepts or ideas. The topic of a typical instructive speech would be: what makes the sky blue? These speeches can be thought of as informal class lectures. In order to deliver an instructive speech effectively, you should try to choose a subject that will be either useful or interesting to your listeners. Following are samples of instructive speeches:

Ideas of Thoreau	Solar energy
The chromatic scale	What controls the tide?
Nuclear submarines	Genetically modified corn

SPEECHES TO REVIEW   Reviews of current books, documentaries, television shows, or plays can provide effective material for an informative speech. Choose one that you feel you are qualified to analyze and explain and that will be interesting to your listeners.

GUIDELINES FOR INFORMATIVE SPEAKING

To communicate effectively, you must have the attention of your audience. In fact, without attention, communication does not exist. Listeners will not pay attention for long to a speech that is neither clear nor interesting. The following are specific suggestions.

Listed next are eight suggestions for making your informative speeches clear and interesting:

1. Practice your speech exactly as you plan to deliver it. If you are showing how to use a juicer, work with the vegetables and fruit in practice just as you would in front of an audience. This will enable you to time your speech accurately. (It might take you longer to prepare and juice the ingredients than you originally thought it would.)
2. Determine whether the audience will see the usefulness of your information. If it is not obvious to your audience that they have something to

gain from paying attention to your demonstration, tell why your information will be useful to them during your introduction.

3. Break your speech down into units or steps so that it can be more easily followed by your audience.

4. Preview the steps you are going to follow in your introduction and summarize them in your conclusion. If your demonstration is long or complicated, consider a review of what has been covered during the body of your speech.

5. Provide continuity to your discussion by talking throughout. Don't be like one young student who began her speech by saying, "Today I'm going to show you how to make Swedish meatballs," and then proceeded to make them without saying another word for the next 3 min. Her meatballs were excellent; her speech was not.

6. Make sure that what you are showing the audience can easily be seen by all. Keep in mind that you must reach the entire audience, not just those in front. If you are not sure your demonstration can easily be seen, estimate the distance from your farthest listener and have a friend take a similar position to check visibility.

7. Maintain your cool. If you make a mistake, acknowledge it and go on. Your audience will appreciate the fact that you admitted your error.

8. Conform to a predetermined time limit for your speech. Before your speech, you decide what you want to show your audience and how much time you want to spend doing it. Don't change that during your delivery.

Make Your Material Clear

The purpose of informative speaking is to add to a listener's understanding. In order to do this, a speaker must communicate clearly. You can help make your material clear by using words that are familiar and specific and by using descriptive gestures.

USE FAMILIAR WORDS   Be assured, unless your listener understands the message, communication will not take place. Sometimes speakers are so concerned with impressing their audience with their vocabularies that they actually fail to communicate. This can be a serious mistake. Unlike the reader who can re-read an unclear passage or look up unfamiliar words, the listener misses part of the message unless the words the speaker uses are understood instantly. Therefore, when you choose your words as a speaker, always choose those that are the most familiar.

USE SPECIFIC WORDS   An effective way of making your ideas clear to others is to use specific language. To say that a person entered the room gives your listener little information. To say that they strutted, ambled, staggered, crept, or marched says it more clearly. The word *tree* is general. *Fruit tree* is more specific. But *Bartlett pear, Courtland apple,* and *Bing cherry* are much more specific and therefore much clearer.

Sometimes a difficult concept can be made clear by explaining it in specific terms. Many people, for example, are unaware of the danger involved in improper disposal of nuclear waste. The student who began her speech, "Even though the dosages would be microscopic so that you couldn't even see them, if 2 pounds of plutonium could be evenly distributed among the world's population, each person on earth would receive a lethal dosage," used the specific to give her audience a better understanding as to the magnitude of the problem.

USE DESCRIPTIVE GESTURES   Descriptive gestures aid by giving your audience a clearer picture of something. You might gesture to show your audience a proper golf swing or to give them an idea of the size of the tomatoes you grew. Or you might give your audience a clear picture of how effective karate can be for self-defense by demonstrating different karate techniques with a volunteer. Descriptive gestures not only make your ideas clearer, they also aid in maintaining audience's interest.

Make Your Delivery Interesting

You must have the attention of your listeners if you want to communicate anything to them. Emphasis and variety will help to hold their attention by making your material as interesting as possible.

EMPHASIS   We emphasize our ideas in speech nonverbally and verbally. An upward inflection and an increase in volume often indicate great enthusiasm. You can tell when people are concerned by the intensity with which they say things. Tone of voice can emphasize, as can pause.

Besides being descriptive, gestures also emphasize. A positive movement of the hands or arms or a nod of the head may emphasize an idea or a point you are making. Leaning or moving toward your audience suggests interest or emphasis. Remember, gestures must be seen to be effective. A good rule of thumb is, "the larger the audience, the broader the gesture."

Another way to emphasize your ideas is to preview and summarize them. List the points you are going to make or steps you are going to follow in your introduction and summarize them in your conclusion.

VARIETY   Most of us prefer to listen to a speaker with a pleasant, conversational style, one who seems to talk with you rather than to you. The key to the conversational style is speaking in a natural manner. It is always a good idea to have a short personal story in your informative speech that doesn't require any notes. When you tell that story, your "real" voice, the one you use everyday is sure to come out and engage the audience.

The next time you are engaged in enthusiastic conversation with your friends, make note of their speech patterns, gestures, and facial expressions. If you can transfer your animation and physical expression in informal conversation to public speaking, you will be more interesting, engaging, and enjoyable as a speaker.

SAMPLE SPEECH TO INFORM

Here is a sample speech to inform on the impact of mental illness on a victim and her family.

MENTAL ILLNESS CAN BE DEVASTATING

Introduction

After working for 9 months as a clerk in a shoe store, my sister, Ellen, told her boss that she had a mental illness. The new medication she was taking was causing nausea, and although her doctor assured her that this would soon pass, she felt she should explain why she was losing time from work. She thought she had a good relationship with her boss, who seemed sympathetic when she told him, but 4 days later, at the end of the week, she was laid off. In the 3 years since that incident, Ellen has worked successfully as a waitress and a secretary, but she no longer speaks of her illness to anyone except her family and closest friends. (attention step)

During the last 4 years, because of my sister, Ellen, I've learned a lot about mental illness. (indicates qualifications) I've learned how scary it is for both the victims and their loved ones. When Ellen was diagnosed with schizophrenia, neither she nor our family knew how to deal with it. It took time but we learned; we learned a lot—and we found out that mental illness can be devastating, but for many recovery is possible. (central idea)

Because mental illness can happen to anyone in this audience at any time and at any age, I'd like to share some of what I've learned with you. (gives reason for listening)

I've divided my speech into five main points that I believe will answer the following questions that most people ask about mental illness: (1) Who gets mental illness? (2) What do people know about it? (3) Why is there stigma attached to it? (4) Are there organizations that can help? (5) Is adequate research and treatment available? (preview main ideas to be covered)

Body

The first question is: Who gets mental illness? Mental illness can happen to anyone at any age; no one is immune. One out of four families in this country is affected by it. Any one of you in this audience could be affected. My sister was diagnosed with schizophrenia when she was 19. Her psychiatrist has mentally ill patients who are as young as 5. Mike Wallace, the newscaster, was stricken with a mental illness in his 60s. Mental illnesses are more common than cancer, diabetes, and heart disease. In any given year, 5 million American adults suffer from an acute episode of one of five serious brain disorders: schizophrenia, bipolar disorder, major depression, obsessive–compulsive disorder, and panic disorder. More than 3 million of America's children suffer from these disorders. People with mental illness utilize more hospital beds than cancer, heart disease, and lung ailments combined.

Question two: What do people know about it? As I told you before, Ellen and the rest of us didn't know what to do because we knew nothing about mental illness. We talked to some mental health professionals, navigated through the Web, picked up some books and brochures on mental illness, and started to learn as much as we could. It soon became apparent to us that when our friends and relatives found out about Ellen, they lacked knowledge and understanding about mental illness, too. However, that didn't stop them from giving advice. Some of them thought that Ellen's schizophrenia was a problem caused by bad parenting. Others thought that she might have gotten into mind-altering drugs. A few suggested that we try tough love to straighten her out. None of them understood that mental illness is a medical condition like diabetes or heart disease requiring treatment, love, and support. The fact is: Most people have little understanding or knowledge of mental illness.

Question three: Why is a stigma attached to mental illness? Ignorance and misinformation are the main sources of the stigma about mental illness. Unfortunately, people incorrectly use terms such as psycho and mental to label those with biological brain disorders. Yet the treated mentally ill are no different than the rest of the population. According to the National Institute of Mental Health, 8 out of 10 mentally ill people can function productively if they receive proper treatment. How many of you in the audience know some people who are mentally ill and can function productively because of the medications they are taking? I'll bet that all of you do but are not aware of it.

For example, you might be surprised to find out that Dick Clark, Bette Midler, Kirk Douglas, Marlon Brando, Patty Duke, Dick Cavett, and Sting are a few of the celebrities who have suffered from mental illness. While some of you didn't know that, I'll bet that many of you do know that John Wayne and Steve McQueen had cancer. Cancer is a horrible disease, but you don't have to be ashamed that you have it. People who have a mental illness often don't admit it because of the stigma attached to it. Kirk Douglas explains it this way: "Why is it that most of us can talk openly about the illnesses of our bodies, but when it comes to our brain and illnesses of the mind, we clam up? And because we clam up, people with emotional disorders feel ashamed and stigmatized, and don't seek the help that can make the difference." The answer to question three is: There is a great deal of stigma attached to mental illness. In the area of stigma, there is much work to be done.

Question four: Are there organizations that can help? There are organizations in every state that you can go to for help. The first months were very stressful for Ellen and the rest of the family, but things got better when we joined the National Alliance for the Mentally Ill (NAMI). NAMI is a national organization with more than 1,200 county and local affiliates in every one of the 50 states, Canada, Puerto Rico, and the Virgin Islands. At NAMI meetings, we learn a lot about mental illness, the latest advances in research and treatment, what is being done to fight stigma and discrimination, what help is available for victims and families, and so on. Ellen attended NAMI meetings, too, and the NAMI clubhouse was where she met new friends and could hang out. At NAMI we can get together with others who have mentally ill loved ones and share our stories of successes and failures and give each other support. Quite a few other places offer help to the mentally ill and their loved ones. To help you find them, NAMI has a toll-free help line. I've put the number on the board. It is 1–800–950–6264. They will put a caller in touch with the closest NAMI affiliate or another organization that can help.

The last question: Is adequate research and treatment available? Research and treatment offer new hope for recovery from mental illness. They've learned a lot about mental illness in the last 12 years—much more than they learned in a thousand years before that. Research organizations like National Association for Research on Schizophrenia and Depression, NARSAD, have made dramatic breakthroughs in the areas of medication and treatment that offer significant hope to victims of this terrible brain disorder. NAMI was one of the founders of NARSAD. Because of organizations like NARSAD that fund research in universities and medical research institutions, giant strides have been made in both research and treatment of biological brain disorders. Newer classes of medications can better treat individuals with severe mental illnesses with far fewer side effects.

Conclusion

Well, I hope that you now have a better understanding of mental illness and what is being done in this country to deal with it. I hope that none of you will become members of the 25% of American families that are affected by it, but if it happens, at least you'll know what you're in store for and have some idea of where you can find help.

As I stand here speaking to you today there are researchers working on new medications and treatments in universities and medical research institutions throughout the world. New psychotropic drugs are being tested right now. The cure for mental illness is out there. Someone has to find it and someone will. You can count on it. Remember, first, mental illness can happen to anyone at any age—no one is immune. Second, most people have little knowledge or understanding of mental illness. Third, there is a great deal of stigma attached to this biological brain disorder. Fourth, there are organizations that help those who are affected to deal with mental illness. And, fifth, new discoveries in research and treatment offer greater hope for recovery. We start the 21st century with better treatment for mental illness and more help available. Remember, mental illness affects one out of four families, but there is hope. Mental illness can be devastating, but for many, recovery is possible.

The prior speech does a great job at conveying well-organized and reasoned information in a clear and engaging manner. Listening to (reading) the presentation, you can imagine how compelled the audience would have been at this presentation assuming the speaker was able to make strong eye contact and use a confident voice. As you construct your own informative speech, try to select a topic that will have personal experiences and stories for you to pull from. After all, information is all around us; but compelling, well-delivered information is a bit more of a rare commodity.

DISCUSSION QUESTIONS

1. What choices should the speaker make so that the information given is easy to understand?
2. What does adding emphasis and variety do for a presentation?
3. Describe the different methods we can employ to keep an informative speech interesting.

EXERCISES

1. Select an informative speech topic for each of the following: demonstration, description, and explanation.
2. How do you think the delivery of information has changed over the last 10 years?
3. After reading the transcript of a speech on mental illness (sample speech to inform), assess some of the ways the presentation engaged the audience.

10 Persuasion

The strongest power that public speaking possesses is the power to persuade. Persuasion in many ways is one of the most powerful tools of life. Persuasion, at its root, is the reason that tanks, machine guns, and aircraft carriers are in existence. They weren't manufactured to shoot, kill, or survive attack as much as they were for their end goal: to persuade. When you think of wars, and life lost in its pursuit, the end goal is usually a signing of a treaty and the bloodshed sadly was a by-product to get the signature. Persuasion is a core human power, and it is important to not to lose sight of the importance.

Persuasion of course occurs in many other avenues that are less confrontational. When you think of persuasion, perhaps you reminisce on a great Super Bowl halftime advertisement. Perhaps you picture a political candidate and his or her campaign promises with hopes of getting elected. Or you may think of a persuasive car salesperson hoping to score a good commission check.

We are involved with persuasion daily as both receivers and senders. We are constantly being bombarded with messages to "get with it," to "enjoy life," and to give ourselves "the very best," all which hope to change our view relating to something. We spend a lot of our time talking to others trying to get them to act a certain way, to agree with our point of view, or just simply to like us more.

The two main differences between this one-to-one persuasion and delivering a persuasive speech are that the speech involves talking to more people and spending more time and effort in planning, preparation, and delivery. Otherwise, the methods are basically the same.

PERSUASION DEFINED

Persuasion can be defined as *a deliberate attempt to influence, reinforce, or change the thought or behavior of others*. Let us examine this definition in detail.

First, consider the word *deliberate*. You must know that your purpose is to persuade. The more aware you are of exactly what you wish to accomplish, the more likely you are to be successful. An informative speech may also persuade, but if its primary purpose is to inform, then the persuasion is accidental.

The second word to remember is *attempt*. Whether you are successful or not, you are still involved in persuasion. The vacuum cleaner salesperson can make a good living delivering the same sales pitch to 10 customers a day, even though only 2 or 3 of them buy the product.

The third important word is *influence*. You don't have to sell the product immediately to be a successful persuader. Persuasion can be a long-range process, which influences thought or behavior a little at a time. Consider, for example, an attempt to improve the image that minority residents of a major city have of the police department. You can't expect to change overnight attitudes that for some it took years to develop. The best you might be able to expect from some of these citizens is to make them a little less antagonistic toward the police.

Persuasion and the Speaker

Over 2,000 years ago, the Greek philosopher Aristotle said that no other factor was more important to success in persuasion than the audience's perception of a persuader as having good sense, good moral character, and goodwill. Speech experts agree that this principle is as true today as it was then. No factor is more important to your success as a persuader than the image your listener has of you as a person. Ideally, you want your audience to see you as a competent person who has integrity and goodwill toward them. If they do, your chances of being successful as a persuader are excellent.

COMPETENCE   Competence means being well qualified, having good sense, and knowing what you are talking about. Most of us are influenced by those who are capable. When we have problems with our electronic equipment, we take it to an expert to have it fixed. When our dentist tells us that we need a root canal, we set up an appointment. When our doctor tells us that our appendix must be removed immediately, we agree.

To be an effective persuader, you must project an image of competence to your audience. To a great extent, this will depend on how much time and effort you put into preparing and delivering your speech. A carefully organized, clearly worded speech is the mark of a competent communicator. Following are five specific suggestions you can use to project an image of competence to your audience:

1. Articulate your words clearly and use correct grammar and pronunciation.
2. Be up-to-date. A relevant speaker uses the most current information available.

3. Tell why you are qualified. If you have education or experience that provides you with special knowledge about your subject, indicate this during your introduction.
4. Speak with confidence. One of the characteristics of the competent person is a positive approach.
5. Be fluent and smooth. Practice your speech so that you can deliver it easily and naturally.

INTEGRITY   Have you ever had the feeling that a politician you were listening to was just a little too smooth, or that even though you couldn't put your finger on it, something made you wonder if you could trust a particular salesperson? Before an audience will accept your ideas, they must feel that you are worthy of their trust and respect. Following are specific suggestions that will help you indicate to your audience that you are sincere and honest:

1. Dress appropriately. Your chances of achieving a positive response will be greater if you dress according to the expectations of your audience.
2. Establish a common bond. Listeners are more inclined to respond positively to a speaker they see as having similar attitudes, values, and experiences.
3. Be objective. To be effective, you must show your audience that you are presenting your views fairly and fully.
4. Indicate your motives. If you have strong motives for presenting your viewpoint, indicate these to your audience. Even if they don't agree with you, they will admire your convictions.
5. Be sincere. You are more likely to project an image of sincerity if your tone of voice and facial expression are appropriate to what you are saying.

GOODWILL   "The key to success for a salesman is to be well liked," says Willie Loman in Arthur Miller's play *Death of a Salesman*. While this is an oversimplification, being well liked is an important qualification for a salesperson. People are much more apt to buy something from someone they like than from someone they are indifferent to or don't like. Therefore, one of your most important jobs as a persuader is to get your audience to like you. The best way to do this is to show that you like them. Here are some specific suggestions you can use to enhance your image as a person of goodwill:

1. Show enthusiasm. Greeting your audience in a lively, energetic way will show them that you are interested in them and happy to be there.
2. Use tact. You can project an image of goodwill by being diplomatic and flexible, especially when dealing with an issue to which some of your listeners are opposed.
3. Be respectful. Treat your listeners with courtesy. Give them credit for having ability, uniqueness, and intelligence.

4. Use humor. An attitude of friendliness is projected by a speaker's use of humor. When used effectively, humor causes both the speaker and the audience to relax.
5. Establish rapport. *Rapport* is a French word meaning "to bring harmony." You can establish rapport with your audience by showing that you like them. Whenever you can, make reference to those in your audience. If you are on a first-name basis with some, refer to them whenever it suits the occasion.

IMAGE In persuasion, the term *image* refers to a mental picture that a customer has of the product that the persuader is selling. That product can be political candidates, a company, a brand of wine, and so on. When you deliver a persuasive speech, the *product* you are selling is you. As you have seen, you want your listeners to have a mental picture of you as a person of competence, integrity, and goodwill. If they do, the chances that they will believe your message will increase.

CREDIBILITY There is a positive relationship between image and credibility: the better the image, the better the credibility. Conversely, a person with a poor image has low credibility. The strength of personal proof can clearly be demonstrated by examining the image–credibility relationship of Dr. Martin Luther King, Jr. As a highly educated, renowned speaker and writer, this national figure projected an image of competence. As a Baptist minister, civil rights leader, and winner of the Nobel Peace Prize, he projected an image of integrity. And as a leader who was so close to his followers that he marched with them, slept with them, and went to jail with them, he projected an image of goodwill. Among his supporters, King's credibility was so high that many of them risked harassment, jail, personal injury, and even their lives to follow him.

The Psychology of Persuasion

The act of persuasion is psychologically based. We tend to act in certain ways because of two factors: attitude and motive. Attitude often determines the way we are going to act, and motive supplies the impulse or desire to act.

ATTITUDES Attitudes are learned. We form them from our education and experience and from our interaction with others. For example, we form favorable or unfavorable attitudes about government, religion, abortion, communism, sex, and so on. These attitudes give direction to our behavior causing us to act in predisposed ways in different situations.

MOTIVES The inner drive or impulse that stimulates behavior is called *motive*. There are two basic types of motives: physical motives and social motives.

Physical Motives Often referred to as basic human drives, physical motives are common to people of all societies. All of us are born with the same basic physiological needs. We want to eat when hungry, drink when thirsty, defend ourselves when threatened, seek safety from the weather, and so on. For many of us in the United States, these basic needs are being abundantly satisfied. And the more money we have, the more we spend to achieve the greatest possible comfort. We buy central air conditioning, contour furniture, and heated swimming pools to pamper our most priceless possession, ourselves. We are, to a great extent, creatures of the body. Although it is unlikely that you will encounter a situation where your listeners have not satisfied their physical needs, making them aware of those who have not can often be quite effective.

Social Motives   A baby is born with a set of physical motives but without social motives. These are learned. No doubt the first social motive the infant develops is the security motive. This motive is primary to the newborn baby and continues as a powerful need at least until the child goes off to school. The tendency of little children to cuddle up; carry a doll, teddy bear, or security blanket around; or hide behind mother when a stranger comes to the door are all examples of the strength of this motive in the small child.

Another motive that develops during this period of closeness to the mother is the approval motion. The baby soon learns that cooing, smiling, laughing, and the like win approval. The child also soon finds that while some things win a pat on the back, others result in a pat on the backside. Approval becomes an important need for the child. For some children the need for approval is so strong that isolation becomes a significant punishment. Banishing a child to their room with the comment "Go to your room. I don't want to see you any more today" can be devastating for some. During this time, children also develop their own attitudes of approval or disapproval toward themselves.

SPECIFIC MOTIVE APPEALS

Sex   Perhaps no motive is appealed to more often in persuasion than the sex motive. Advertising in this country is supersaturated with sex to sell everything from shock absorbers to perfume. Automobiles, cigarettes, toothpaste, and diet sodas are all used by young, vibrant, *beautiful* people, and if you use these products, somehow you will be beautiful too. Be assured, the sex motive plays an important role in all areas of persuasion.

Security   Another appeal often used in advertising is the security motive. The effect that this motive has on us and our loved ones is clearly evident in today's society. We have banks to protect our money, unions to protect our jobs, and insurance companies to provide for our health care, and when the time comes, for our survivors.

We go to college to provide for a more secure future, we "go steady" to ensure a dependable date, and we put money aside for a "rainy day." In this age of violence and uncertainty, no generation has been as security minded as this one.

Approval   Whether it be at home, at work, at school, or among friends, we are constantly seeking the approval of others. Any advertisement that features brand names is selling approval along with the product. A person might spend months landscaping a backyard or painting a picture for the satisfaction of being able to say, "I made this myself."

Conformity   Closely related to the approval motive is the motive to conform. Even in the most primitive societies, people have customs, morals, and rules to which they must conform in order to live in harmony with their peers. Most people tend to go along with the group rather than swim against the stream. Have you ever, for example, worn a style that was not particularly becoming to you because it was the thing to do? Or would you dare show up in jeans at a formal dance?

Success   The desire to succeed can be a powerful motive. For some, it is so intense that it overshadows all others. Individuals have been so strongly motivated to succeed that they have lied, cheated, and even killed to further this ambition. Advertisers have used the success motive to sell products ranging from toothpaste to condominiums. The success motive has long been used to sell luxury cars. People who buy Mercedes, Cadillacs, Porsches, and Lexus are buying success along with the automobile.

Creativity   Creativity is one of the motives that can be unusually forceful. Some have spent years of self-sacrifice and deprivation in an attempt to develop an artistic or musical ability. Who hasn't heard of a starving artist's sale or an author who could paper a room with rejection slips from publishers? The fact that these people continue creating testifies to the strength of this motive. At other times, motives are in conflict with each other. Take, for example, the person who attends a party where drugs are being used. To refuse to go along with the group can threaten that person's popularity and peer approval, but to use the drugs can be a threat to security and parental approval. As you can see, motives have a significant impact on people's lives.

Reasoning and the Persuasive Process

Reasoning is the process of drawing conclusions from evidence. There are two kinds of evidence: evidence of fact and evidence of opinion. The explanation of this reasoning process to others in an attempt to influence belief is called *argumentation*. A basic argument consists of two statements: a premise and a conclusion drawn from that premise. Here are two basic arguments:

1. Mark is a member of a gang. Therefore, he is a troublemaker.
2. Mark has been arrested 3 times. Therefore, he is a troublemaker.

Both statements involve a premise–conclusion relationship. In the first example, the conclusion is drawn from the fact that Mark is a member of a gang. "Mark is a member of a gang. Therefore, he is a troublemaker." This argument is based on deductive reasoning. You have come to the conclusion that Mark is a troublemaker because he belongs to a gang. You reason from a general premise (members of a gang are troublemakers) to a minor premise (Mark is a member of a gang) to the conclusion (therefore, Mark is a troublemaker). Whenever you reason from a general rule to a specific case, you are reasoning deductively.

The second statement, "Mark has been arrested 3 times. Therefore, he is a troublemaker," is an example of inductive reasoning. There is no rule to guide the reasoner, only the observation about Mark: He has been arrested 3 times. Therefore, he is a troublemaker. When you come to a conclusion as the result of observing or experiencing individual situations or cases, you are using inductive reasoning. Although you may not have been aware of it, you have used this form of reasoning throughout your life. Do you like pizza? Enjoy rock music? Think that you are a good student? Whether your answer to these questions is yes or no, it has undoubtedly been based on inductive reasoning. You probably decided whether you liked pizza after eating one, three, five, or more. The same was true about your attitude toward rock music and your status as a student. Your observation or experience with these involvements has determined your conclusion.

Reasoning by Generalization

This type of reasoning involves examining specific details or examples and coming to a general conclusion. If there are a limited number of instances involved, the more you cite, the more probable are the conclusions. For example, you might argue that Senator Jones is prolabor and Senator Smith antilabor by citing their voting records on legislation affecting labor.

When used well, generalization can be an effective argument in persuasion. Carefully controlled scientific experiments and studies can provide strong evidence for your speeches.

Reasoning by Comparison

Argument by comparison involves the examination of two similar cases. If the two have enough similarities, it is possible to argue that what is true of one case will be true of the others as well. The comparisons may be either literal or figurative. Literal comparisons compare things that are within the same categories, such as the U.S. inflation rates in 2012 and 2013 and a comparison of academic standards at different universities. If the similarities in the literal comparisons are significant, the conclusions often appear logical.

Reasoning from Cause and Effect

Causal reasoning is based on the principle that every cause has an effect. When two things occur together with any frequency, we might naturally determine that one is caused by the other. For example, the person who complains, "Every time I eat pizza, I get heartburn," might logically assume that the pizza has triggered the heartburn. However, since cause-and-effect relationships can often be quite complicated, it could be that the heartburn is caused by a gallbladder disorder, which is aggravated by eating the pizza, so that rather than giving up pizza, the person should see a doctor.

Causal relationships are most clearly demonstrated in carefully controlled situations. For example, a number of years ago, researchers were interested in finding out what effect music had on the milk production of dairy cows. They used two experimental groups and a control group. Each group of cows was housed in the same size barn, fed the same food, and matched in every relevant way, except that after the first week, light classical music was piped into barn A, hard rock into barn B, and no music into barn C. The results of the experiment, which ended after week 2, were that group A produced half again as much milk as they had during week 1, group B's production was reduced by one-third, and group C's production remained the same. The experiment showed clearly what effect the music had on the cows.

Keep in mind that causal relationships are more difficult to identify in less controlled situations. This is especially true in political, economic, and social situations, which frequently have multiple causes.

FALLACIES

Fallacies are an error in reasoning. Some fallacies occur so often that they have been isolated and labeled. The most common of these are treated next.*

Hasty Generalization

Hasty generalizations is the most readily available fallacy. It happens when conclusions are based on insufficient or unfair evidence, or when it is not warranted by the facts available. For example, "All hippies are dirty," "All welfare recipients are lazy," and so on.

False Cause

False cause fallacy occurs when there is no logical relationship between a cause and an effect. Thus, you might conclude that the Democratic party promotes war, that television viewing increases juvenile delinquency, and that gambling creates poverty. With the fallacy reasoning, there is no definitive link between the first point and its relation to the second point.

Begging the Question

An argument begs the question when it assumes something as true when it actually needs to be proven. For instance, the declaration that "these corrupt laws must be changed" asserts the corruption but does not prove it, and consequently the conclusion is not justified.

Begging the question also occurs when we make a charge and then insist that someone else disprove it. For example, to answer the question "How do

---

*This section is taken with permission from Arthur Koch and Stanley B. Felber, *What Did You Say?* 3rd ed. (Upper Saddle River, NJ: Prentice-Hall, 1985).

you know that the administration is honest?" would put the respondent in the position of trying to disprove a conclusion that was never proven in the first place. Remember, whoever makes an assertion has the burden of proof.

Ignoring the Question

Ignoring the question occurs when the argument shifts from the original subject to a different one, or when the argument appeals to some emotional attitude that has nothing to do with the logic of the case. An example of the first would be a man replying "Haven't you ever done anything dishonest?" when accused of cheating on his wife. He ignores the question of his infidelity by shifting to a different argument.

An argument that appeals to the emotional attitudes of the reader or listener would be the statement "No good American would approve of this communistic proposal."

False Analogy

When reasoning concludes what is true in one case is also true in another, false analogy is employed. "George will do well in graduate school; he had an excellent academic record as an undergraduate." Unfortunately, graduate school and undergraduate success are two completely different obstacles and this reasoning is false. "There's nothing to handling a snowmobile; it's just like riding a bicycle," again shows how two dissimilar activities can be lumped together as one process.

Either/or Fallacy

The either/or fallacy is reasoning that concludes there are only two choices to an argument when there are other possible alternatives. A tragic example would be the reasoning that escalated the Vietnam War. The argument was: Either we fight and win in Vietnam or all of Southeast Asia will fall to the Communists. Of course, we didn't win and all of Southeast Asia didn't fall to the Communists.

Ad Hominem

In this fallacy, the argument shifts from the real issue to attacking the person. Unfortunately, this abuse often occurs in politics, and the voters who fall for it wind up casting their votes against a candidate rather than for one. "I wouldn't trust him. He cheated on his wife," or "You're not going to believe a former convict?" are examples of this fallacy that direct the attention away from where actual emphasis should be placed.

Red Herring

The red herring is similar to the ad hominem fallacy but does not attack the opponent's character. It gets its name from the superstition that if you drag a red herring across your path, it will throw any wild animals following you off the track. Information is introduced that is not relevant to the question at hand in the hope that it will divert attention from the real issue. In politics, an opposing candidate is pictured as being overly religious, ultrarich, or divorced. If the trait has nothing to do with the way he will perform in office, the argument is a red herring.

Bandwagon

The bandwagon argument appeals to the theory that whatever the masses believe is true. Have you ever heard someone say, "Yes, I think that is the direction to head—everyone else agrees with it right?" Make no mistake, popularity is not always an accurate determiner of truth.

TYPES OF PERSUASIVE SPEECHES

Persuasive speeches can be classified into three types: (1) speeches to convince; (2) speeches to reinforce; and (3) speeches to activate. Careful audience analysis is essential in persuasive speaking. The type of persuasion a speaker chooses should be based on the attitudes of the audience before the speech and the specific changes sought.

Speeches to Convince

At times a persuader must deal with an audience that is either undecided, indifferent, or opposed to a proposition.

The president defending his healthcare plan, a college debater attempting to prove that capital punishment is desirable, and a student senate leader trying to convince fellow students that the student senate is doing a good job are all cases of persuasion to convince.

Because speeches to convince appeal to the listener's intelligence rather than emotions, they employ logical rather than psychological or personal appeals. They must rely on clear reasoning and carefully selected evidence in order to get listeners to respond satisfactorily.

Speeches to Reinforce

Rather than appealing to their intelligence, a speech to reinforce appeals essentially to the motives, attitudes, and sentiments of an audience. Rather than being undecided, indifferent, or opposed, the audience is in agreement with the speaker's point of view.

On Veterans Day, a speaker reminds the audience of the sacrifices made by those who fought and died so that each of them might enjoy this land of freedom. Those in the audience already believe that the sacrifices made by these veterans were important. However, the speaker wants to strengthen that belief, to reinforce that appreciation, to deepen that concern.

The Independence Day orator, the speaker at a pep rally, the commencement speaker, the political speaker at the Democratic National Convention, and the persons delivering eulogies, inaugural addresses, memorials, and testimonials are involved with persuasion to reinforce. Their purpose is to strengthen the existing attitudes, sentiments, emotions, and beliefs of their audience.

Speeches to Activate

The speech to activate calls for a specific action on the part of the audience. It asks them to buy, to join, to march, to sign. A speech to convince may attempt to create an awareness in the audience as to the danger to our society caused by easy access to handguns; the speech to activate seeks to get those in the audience to write to their representatives in Congress urging them to vote to get handguns off the streets. A speech to reinforce may seek to arouse greater concern for the plight of the hungry in our society; the speech to activate would seek an overt response, asking the audience for a specific donation of food or money to respond directly to the problem.

While the speech to activate may employ the logical and psychological appeals used in speeches to convince and reinforce, the purpose of this speech is to get a specific action. For this reason, speeches to activate are generally more successful when directed at audiences that basically agree with the speaker's point of view.

DISCUSSION QUESTIONS

1. What is the difference between informative speeches and persuasive speeches?
2. What are the nine fallacies discussed in the chapter? Have you seen any of these fallacies surface in your life?
3. Discuss and describe the three methods of reasoning.

EXERCISES

1. Watch a persuasive speech on Youtube.com and discuss the method of persuasion employed in the speech.
2. Analyze a persuasive speech or sales pitch you have been subject to and write out the tactics of their persuasion and whether the messages worked as planned.
3. Create a sample commercial or print advertisement for a product that you are familiar with and like. What type of appeals do you need to persuade your audience that this is a good product?

11 Group Communication

Functioning within a small group is part of the American culture. Nearly all Fortune 500 companies have adopted this method into their workforce. Understanding the dynamics of groups and the impact of your own behavior within a group is critical to your success in the workforce and in life.

If you are like most people, you participate in some form of group discussion almost daily. There are all kinds of group discussions. They may be planned or spontaneous, structured or unstructured, formal or informal, permanent or temporary. Some discussions take place with a group of friends over coffee or with fellow workers during the lunch hour. Others occur in the home where everything from the high cost of living to what to do about the neighbor's dog may be covered. More and more, however, discussions are occurring more formally in organized committees and action groups.

During the last two decades citizens have become increasingly involved in the affairs of their communities. Organizations like MADD (Mothers Against Drunk Driving) and CUB (Citizens' Utility Board) have sprung up as a result of people demanding to have a voice in determining policies that affect their lives. In addition, many strong organizational groups have formed to assess the status quo such as the Occupy Wall Street movement, the revolutions in Egyptian and Tunisia, as well as the Tea Party movement. What these groups have in common is the sum of the parts is greater than each individual member. In other words, $1 + 1 + 1 = 8$. The additional 5 added to the previous equation takes in to account the concept of synergy, or when the whole is greater than the individuals.

It is because of synergy that so many companies utilize groups to solve problems. Companies tend to not like spending extra money where it may not be useful, and by group problem solving being such a dominant theme it is clear that groups, and the synergy they create, are useful in both creating creative ideas and value.

For the blending ideas and content to happen in groups, there has to be the exchange of information. Discussions do just that: they exchange information between members. Discussion has been a vital part of your formal education. Many instructors employ a lecture–discussion format, and group discussion is often used in classes to promote learning. The advantages of becoming a group participant in discussions are obvious: you learn the material better; you get more context and unique angles of understanding the information; and you actually retain the information much more clearly.

THE FUNCTIONS OF DISCUSSION

In general, discussion has four functions: social, educative, therapeutic, and problem solving.

Social Discussion

Social discussion usually occurs spontaneously and is temporary, unstructured, and informal. A typical example of social discussion would be a group of students sitting around a table in the student union, discussing the federal government's focus on only funding colleges that keep tuition increases to a minimum. Another example might be a group of businesspeople discussing federal budget cuts from an entirely different viewpoint over cocktails at the 19th hole of the local country club. Neither group will resolve the problem they are discussing. However, many of the participants will benefit from the interchange of ideas, the reinforcement of attitudes, and the enjoyment that social discussion groups provide.

Educative Discussion

The function of educative discussion (sometimes called *information-seeking discussion*) is to make you better informed about the topic discussed. Examples of educative discussion groups include garden clubs, Bible study groups, musical societies, and book clubs. One of the most familiar examples of educative discussion is classroom discussion, which is particularly well suited to the speech class. A brief discussion following each classroom speech can provide valuable feedback to both the speaker and the audience. An all-class discussion of the textbook and the exams will help students better understand speech principles and what is expected of them in the class.

Therapeutic Discussion

A third function of discussion is the therapeutic group. The leader of this group is almost always a trained therapist, whose goal is the personal improvement of each member. Examples of therapeutic groups include alcohol and drug rehabilitation groups, marriage counseling groups, religious encounter groups, and weight-watching groups. These provide a supportive atmosphere where individuals can learn why they act the way they do and what they can do to change their behavior.

Problem-Solving Discussion

Group problem solving is superior to individual problem solving for a number of reasons. First, an individual's background and experience can seldom match those of a group. The more people working on a problem, the more information is available to solve it. Second, the more people you have looking at a problem, the more likely you are to solve it correctly. In a group, an error by one individual is likely to be spotted by someone else.

As our society grows increasingly complex, more and more problems that must be dealt with are surfacing. The majority of them will be addressed in problem-solving group discussion. In governmental committee meetings, business conferences, church councils, legislative sessions, classroom meetings, and the like, problems are being solved, policies are being determined, and decisions are being made, which affect the lives of millions of people. As an educated person, you will be called on to participate in a variety of discussion situations. A study of the principles of group communication, together with guided practice, will help you to develop the knowledge and skill necessary for effective participation.

TYPES OF DISCUSSION

Since the discussion groups you participate in will most likely be either educative or problem solving, the rest of this chapter will concentrate only on these. The six basic types of discussion are the roundtable, the panel, the symposium, the lecture forum, the dialogue, and the interview.

The Roundtable

In the roundtable discussion, the participants sit at a round table or in a circle. There are two reasons for this seating arrangement: (1) when seated in a circle, everyone is in a position to maintain eye contact with the others while speaking or listening to them, and (2) no one is seated in a superior "head of the table" position. Each participant is in a position equal to that of his or her neighbor. Everyone, including the moderator or leader if there is one, is involved in a roundtable discussion. There is no audience. This type of discussion is particularly suited to council and committee meetings, conferences, and classroom discussions. Although roundtable discussions usually involve from 3 to 15 members, an effective classroom discussion can be held with as many as 25.

The Panel

A panel usually consists of three to six panelists and a moderator. The members sit in front of an audience or judge in a circle or semicircle so that they can see and react to each other. The language used by panel members is usually informal and conversational. Although panel participants are often made aware of the discussion problem beforehand, most panels are unrehearsed to ensure spontaneity and enthusiasm during the presentation.

Panels that are followed by an audience participation period, or forum, are usually timed. For example, for a 1 hr program, 40 min might be set aside for the panel and 20 min for the forum period. It is the moderator's job to summarize the discussion and field the questions from the audience.

The Symposium

Unlike roundtable and panel discussions, which are like magnified conversations, the symposium consists of a series of prepared speeches, each dealing with a specific aspect of the same topic. The number of speakers for a symposium usually ranges from three to five. A time limit is given to each of the speakers, who talk directly to the audience rather than to each other. The moderator opens the discussion, introduces each speaker and topic, and summarizes the discussion at the conclusion. If there is a forum period following the summary, the moderator fields the questions, rephrasing them when necessary.

The Lecture Forum

The lecture forum involves a moderator and a lecturer who delivers a prepared speech on a subject. The speech is followed by a forum period. The job of the moderator is to introduce the subject and speaker and preside during the forum period. The lecture forum technique has long been used by classroom teachers and political candidates, who then field questions from the audience.

Another variation of the lecture forum is the film forum. The success of this technique is largely dependent on the quality of the film shown and the ability of the moderator to deal effectively with any questions the audience may have regarding the film.

The Dialogue

A dialogue is an interchange and discussion of ideas between two people. It is highly successful when both participants know their subjects well. The dialogue can be a useful classroom exercise. It is an excellent means of communicating information. For best results, the dialogue should be carefully planned so that both participants know where the discussion is heading.

The Interview

A carefully planned interview can be an excellent way to communicate information. In the discussion interview, the participants should plan the questions in advance so both will know where the discussion is going. A good interviewer can elicit a wealth of information from a well-informed interviewee.

Role-Playing

An excellent way to introduce a discussion problem is through the technique of role-playing. In role-playing, the players take part in a brief drama built on a *real-life* problem. The actors in the drama each take the part of a specific character in the problem. They then act out the situation, expressing the views they feel the character they are playing would have. The drama is unrehearsed, and the problem is usually given to the participants on the day the role-playing is to take place.

Role-playing can be an effective way of pretesting a situation. Skill in handling oneself in an interview could make the difference between a student's getting a job and missing it. A series of mock interviews with students playing the roles of personnel director and interviewee provides excellent practice. Students will derive a greater feeling of confidence toward the interview situation and an increased understanding of management's position as well. Role-playing is particularly useful in clarifying a situation. Often, after seeing the roles played, a group can more fully understand the problem.

SELECTING A ROLE-PLAYING PROBLEM   The problems below have been prepared with today's college student in mind. Additional problems may be developed by members of a group in a discussion situation, or by individual students as part of a class assignment.

One final note: After engaging in role-playing these problems, allow time for those in the audience to give their views and reactions to the drama.

1. A student who is of legal age is asked by his friends to buy the liquor for a weekend beach party. He knows he can get charged with contributing to the delinquency of minors if he is caught. He also wants to keep the status he has among his friends. What should the student do?
2. A new employee in a plant has a mother who must have open-heart surgery. She lives in another state, and the employee would like to take a 4 day leave of absence to be with her. The plant is behind in filling orders, and everyone is working a 7 day week. How should the employee handle the situation?
3. The students in an English class feel that the instructor assigns an excessive amount of homework each day. The instructor is teaching the course for the first time. How should the students handle the situation?
4. A student who will graduate in 3 weeks is offered a job that will start on the morning of his last exam. His instructor has indicated that he will give no early or makeup exams. What should the student do?
5. A first-year bank employee has been late for work on an average of 2 or 3 times a week for the last month. His wife, who is in the hospital, will remain there for at least another week. The reason he has been late is that he has to feed, dress, and drive his three school-age children to school each day. His supervisor has called him in to talk about his tardiness. How should the bank employee handle the situation?

PARTICIPATING IN DISCUSSION

To a great extent, successful discussion depends on the participants. Sometimes, discussions fail because the participants have little knowledge of the subject and, consequently, little to offer in solving the problem. At other times, a discussion ends in aimless argument because of the inflexibility or refusal to compromise. Breakdowns in communication, an unfriendly atmosphere, and a tendency to stray from the subject also contribute to the failure of discussion. Effective participation in discussion requires both ability and understanding. Following are the duties of a participant in a discussion.

Listen Carefully

Critical listening is essential to effective discussion. It is an active process requiring both attention and concentration. All too often group members respond to what they *thought* someone meant. If you are unclear as to the meaning of something that was said during a discussion, say so before the discussion continues.

Be Prepared

Every member of a discussion has a responsibility to be well informed on the topic being discussed. This means that if you have little knowledge of the subject, you spend time and effort researching it. If you are delivering a lecture or are a member of a symposium panel, prepare and practice your speech carefully so that you can deliver it extemporaneously with good eye contact.

Be Spontaneous

Participate whenever you have something relevant to say. Although you must not interrupt another speaker, if you have something important to say, interject it when there is a pause in the conversation. A relevant comment in the right place can often save the group time.

Share the Spotlight

Although you should participate when you have a worthwhile contribution, don't monopolize the discussion. Group thinking can be thought of as thinking out loud. Unless all members contribute, the full value of their knowledge and experience will not be brought to bear on the problem.

Be Courteous

The old saying "You catch more flies with honey than with vinegar" is especially appropriate to the group discussion situation. Group discussion requires flexibility and compromise. It is unlikely that either will occur in a hostile atmosphere.

Be Cooperative

Participants in group discussion must put the best interests of the group above their own personal interests. The goal of discussion is to arrive at a solution acceptable to all members of the group. This means that group members must be willing to work cooperatively to avoid conflict.

Be Objective

In order for a discussion to be successful, each member must approach the question in an unbiased, objective way. If for some reason you have a strongly held attitude that would prevent you from discussing a topic objectively, excuse yourself from the discussion group.

Stick to the Point

Few things are more frustrating to a group than when a member introduces material that is completely off the subject. It is every member's responsibility to keep the discussion on track. Always be aware of where the discussion is heading and contribute only when your remarks are pertinent.

Use Time Wisely

A discussion participant should avoid drawing out analysis of a point. Once agreement is reached in regard to some aspect of the problem, move on. To explain to the group why you made the same decision as another member is counter productive.

Speak Concisely

Unless the listener understands the message, communication does not take place. If you want to be understood, articulate your words carefully and pronounce them correctly. Speak with adequate volume and emphasize important points so that the other members of the group know exactly where you stand.

Be Natural

No matter which form of discussion you are involved in, be yourself. Speak in a conversational manner with which you feel comfortable. If you try to change your way of speaking, you are liable to sound stilted and unnatural.

MODERATING THE DISCUSSION

Most discussion forms require a moderator. Seven specific duties of a moderator are listed here:

1. Start the discussion by introducing the topic and the lecturer or discussion participants to the audience.
2. Direct the discussion by seeing to it that the subject is adequately discussed and that the group moves steadily toward a solution or conclusion.

3. Encourage participation. Members who do not take part in the discussion contribute little or nothing to the outcome.
4. Resolve conflicts by using tact and diplomacy to minimize tension.
5. Control the time to make sure all aspects of the problem are discussed.
6. Provide transitions and summaries to help participants see what has been accomplished and what remains to be done.
7. Take charge of the forum period. Field all questions, rephrasing when necessary.

A PATTERN FOR PROBLEM SOLVING

Identifying the Problem

The first step in problem-solving discussion is to have the members pinpoint the problem. Many discussions fail because the problem is not clearly understood by all. Next, the problem must be carefully worded. When wording the problem for discussion, the group should adhere to the following guidelines:

1. The problem should be worded in the form of a question. A properly worded question holds up a problem in such a way as to motivate discussants to seek solutions to it.
2. It should be phrased to avoid a yes or no answer. Participants who answer yes or no to a question often feel committed to defend that answer. The result is that what started out as objective discussion turns into subjective debate.
3. It should be stated in an impartial way. A discussion question should never indicate bias. The question "When will we stop the stupid sale of handguns?" is prejudiced. It would be far better to ask "How can the sale of handguns be effectively regulated?"
4. It should be worded specifically. The question "What should the government do to prevent terrorism?" is far too vague. Which government are we talking about? Where will the terrorism take place? A better question would be "What steps should the federal government take to prevent terrorists from illegally entering the United States?"
5. It should be sufficiently restricted. The question "What should be done to stop world hunger?" is so broad that it could not be adequately covered in a set period of time. A better question would be, "What should be done to stop hunger in Detroit?"

Analyzing the Problem

After identifying and wording the problem, the nature and causes of the problem should be explored. The group should consider such questions as these: What is the history of the problem? How serious is it? Who is affected by it? What are the causes?

The process of analysis usually requires research. Participants should research the discussion problem just as they would research the topic for a speech. A thorough investigation of the problem will give discussants a clear understanding of what conditions need correcting.

The final step in analysis is to decide on guidelines to evaluate proposed solutions. These guidelines should be agreed upon before possible solutions are proposed. A typical list of guidelines might include the following: it must be safe; it must be affordable; it must be obtainable; and it must not create new problems.

Finding the Best Solution

At this point, members of the group should suggest possible solutions. It is a good idea to identify as many solutions as possible before evaluating any of them. An effective way to compile an adequate list of solutions is by using a technique called *brainstorming*.

In a discussion, the brainstorming technique can be handled in two ways. The first is to have members of the group write down whatever solutions come to mind as quickly as they can. They should jot them down in phrases or sentences without evaluating them. After 5 min, the exercise stops, and each list of solutions is read aloud. The second technique has one member of the group proposing a solution, another posing a different one, and so on. The brainstorming continues for a set period of time or until the group has no more solutions to offer. One member should be assigned to write down all the ideas.

Once a list of solutions has been established, the group can quickly eliminate any that are illogical or repetitive. The remaining solutions can then be evaluated according to the guidelines established earlier. It is wise for the group to evaluate each solution on the list before making their choice.

Finally, the group should make every effort to reach agreement as to the best solution or solutions. If they cannot reach a consensus, a majority vote should be taken.

Activating the Solution

Once the group has agreed on a solution, it is necessary to take action. This might mean drafting a letter and sending it to the appropriate representatives in Washington, framing a petition and collecting signatures, or planning and staffing a fund-raising event. Perhaps the proposed solution will take the form of an oral report to the mayor and city council or to your instructor and the rest of the class. Sometimes a solution will require a written report. Whatever action is taken, the last job the group has is to implement the solution it chooses.

DISCUSSION QUESTIONS

1. What are the seven duties of a moderator?
2. If you are participating in a group discussion, which of the 11 outlined duties of the participant are most important?
3. Discuss a group that you belong to and how decisions are addressed, discussed, and decided upon.

EXERCISES

1. Observe a group in action, on campus, in your church, or in your community discussing an issue or decision to be made. Does everyone participate? Are ideas discussed in a friendly cooperative way? Does the group stay on track and discuss the problem in a friendly cooperative way? Is there a moderator? Fill out the discussion rating form and share your views with the class.

2. Try to incorporate the patterns of problem solving into a group in which you were a member. Discuss how you identified the problem, analyzed the problem, and found the best solution.

3. Briefly interview someone who has experience in working in small groups for their employment. What are their opinions? What works well? What could work better? Do they think small group problem solving is useful?

INDEX